SAUDI ARABIA

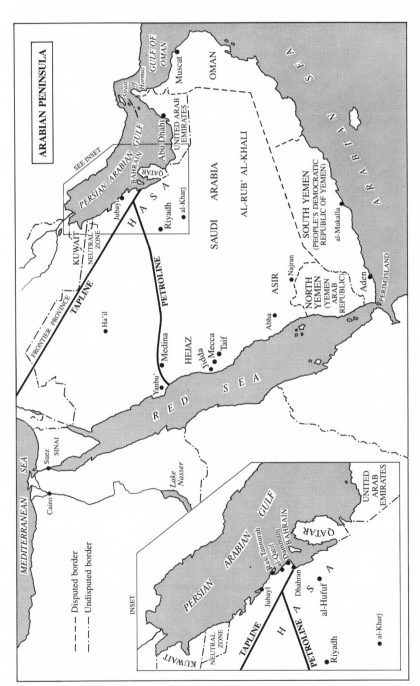

Map of Saudi Arabia

SAUDI ARABIA

THE MAKING OF A FINANCIAL GIANT

ARTHUR N. YOUNG

HEAD OF THE FINANCIAL MISSION, 1951–1952

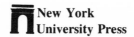New York
University Press

Library of Congress Cataloging in Publication Data

Young, Arthur N. (Arthur Nichols), 1890–
Saudi Arabia

(New York University studies in Near Eastern
civilization ; no. 8)
Includes bibliographical references and index.
1. Mu'assasat al-Naqd al-'Arabī al-Sa'ūdī—
History.   2. Financial institutions—Saudi Arabia—
History.   3. Money—Saudi Arabia—History.   4. Saudi
Arabia—Economic conditions.   I. Title.   II. Series.
HG1213.Y68   1983   332.1'0953'8   82-24569
ISBN 0-8147-9661-3

Manufactured in the United States of America

Clothbound editions of New York University Press books are Smyth-
sewn and printed on permanent and durable acid-free paper.

To
my children
grandchildren and
great-grandchildren

CONTENTS

ILLUSTRATIONS

CHARTS

APPENDIXES

PREFACE

Only the tales of the genie of the *Arabian Nights* could match what has been taking place during the half century since Saudi Arabia's warring tribes were welded into a unified state by Abd al-Aziz—commonly known in the West as King Ibn Saud. Who in the 1920s could have imagined the change from an isolated desert state, which the United States wondered whether to recognize, to the fantastically rich, developing and influential country of today?

In the early days the finance minister, as Sir Reader Bullard put it, could keep the national treasury "in a box under his bed." When the Americans found oil in 1938, total revenue equalled only about $7 million yearly. The currency was the world's hardest: silver and gold coins. But the value of each varied widely both at home and abroad. When oil money began to flow in rapidly after World War II, there was no good way to handle it. Orderly progress was impossible unless means could be found to manage this money, with a convenient and stable currency. Several moves for reform were made. But without success.

In the year 1950 oil revenue grew to $57 million, and that was only the beginning—it was $101 billion in 1981 (equal to about one-sixth of the total revenues of the United States government). The king and his counselors knew they needed outside help. They asked the American government to recommend a Financial Mission. They were ready to take advice. This, with the prospects of large and growing wealth, gave them a rare opportunity to lay the financial foundations of a modern state.

It was my good fortune to be called upon for this work. It was a rare privilege to go to Saudi Arabia in 1951 and to have a part in helping at an important turning point in its history. In particular, it was gratifying to help in the planning and creation of the Saudi Arabian Monetary Agency. Opened in 1952 with capital of $6 million, it has become one of the world's leading financial institutions. Its foreign assets were about $119 billion in the fall of 1981. The constructive result in Saudi Arabia is personally pleasing after the frustration, when financial adviser to China, of seeing most of the constructive work of the 1930s go down the drain during the Sino-Japanese war and its aftermath.

The financial framework put in place in 1952 made possible the transition to a modern financial system. But it was only a framework for progress. There remained the arduous task of moving from a traditional society to what the Covenant of the League of Nations called "the strenuous conditions of the modern world."

This book undertakes to shed light upon the way in which Saudi Arabia's financial institutions and administration rose to the challenges of the past eventful half century, during which this desert realm was transformed into one of the world's leading economic and financial powers.

Arthur N. Young

Claremont, California
June 1982

ACKNOWLEDGMENTS

I am grateful to Professor R. B. Winder, Director of the Hagop Kevorkian Center for Near Eastern Studies of New York University, for helpful advice in the final stages of completing this writing. For reading and criticizing the first draft I was fortunate to have the help of others with firsthand knowledge of the period with which I deal. These persons are Thomas C. Barger, former Chairman of the Arabian American Oil Company (Aramco); William D. Brewer, retired Ambassador and currently head of the Chevalier Program in Diplomacy and World Affairs at Occidental College; Professor George Rentz, Arabist of Johns Hopkins University; and Professor A. J. Meyer, Associate Director of Harvard's Center for Middle East Studies, who encouraged me to do this writing and helped in many ways. For reading and criticizing parts of the draft I am indebted to retired Ambassador William J. Porter and Professor Raymond F. Miksell of the University of Oregon, and to Elizabeth Monroe, distinguished authority on the Middle East.

Also I had valuable help from William Sands, former editor of the *Middle East Journal;* William F. Todd of Aramco; Richard S. Reed of the World Bank; my brother John Parke Young and his wife Marie

Louise Young, both formerly of the State Department; my grandson, Stephen E. Roulac, President of Questor Associates of San Francisco; and Isma'il I Nawwab of Aramco and the editors of *Aramco World Magazine* who provided illustrations. Governor Abd al-Aziz al-Qurayshi of the Saudi Arabian Monetary Agency kindly supplied data and a picture of the Agency's headquarters. The National Energy Information Center of the United States Department of Energy helpfully provided statistics. Finally, Colin H. Jones, Director of New York University Press, Managing Editor Despina Papazoglou, and copyeditor Frank Kirk raised good questions and provided criticism that greatly enhanced the manuscript. Gladys S. Burton faithfully typed the text.

For the work as it stands and any errors and/or omissions, those who have helped me are of course not responsible.

SAUDI ARABIA

1

THE FOUNDING OF
MODERN SAUDI ARABIA

It was in the decades between the two world wars that Saudi Arabia began to change from a land of nomads, oases, and a few walled towns to one of the world's key countries. The major causes of change were the unification of most of Arabia by Abd al-Aziz, commonly known as Ibn Saud, and the discovery of the world's richest oilfields. During less than half a century these events, with the efforts of Saudi Arabia's leaders and people, have had a spectacular effect. They have transformed the country's face, and given Saudi Arabia a place in the world, in a way without precedent in history.

THE RISE TO POWER OF ABD AL-AZIZ

Abd al-Aziz (1880–1953) was born in Riyadh, the ancestral stronghold of descendants of Muhammad ibn Saud. They had long ruled much of Arabia but with some interruptions, such as that during the decade before 1902. In that year Abd al-Aziz, by leading the spectacular capture of Riyadh, began moves that led to uniting the warring tribes. A major factor in the success of Abd al-Aziz was his zeal in propagating the doctrines of the puritanical Wahhabi sect of the Sunni branch of Islam.[1] His drive for unification succeeded only after much fighting and extensive missionary work. His essential procedure was to conquer, proselytize, and form alliances sustained by providing subsidies and often taking as a wife a daughter of a tribal chief. Revenue was gained from both booty taken in the wars and periodic grants from the British.[2]

During World War I and in its immediate aftermath Abd al-Aziz was little known outside the Middle East. Attention centered on the legendary T. E. Lawrence, who backed Husayn ibn Ali. As sharif of Mecca, Husayn ruled the Hijaz, the western region of Arabia that included the holy city of Medina as well as Mecca.

Britain had long held a sphere of influence in the Middle East. After World War I the League of Nations granted Britain a mandate for Palestine and Trans-Jordan, bordering on Arabia, which continued until 1948. Britain also received a mandate for Iraq and had a protectorate over Egypt. The British had a long history of subsidizing rulers in the Middle East. During World War I, when Turkey was an enemy and ruled parts of Arabia, Britain gave substantial aid to Sharif Husayn and provided some aid to Abd al-Aziz in the east, both of whom opposed the Turks.

In these years British policy with regard to the Middle East was poorly coordinated. Relations with western Arabia, the Red Sea area, were carried out through the Arab Bureau in Cairo. This bureau was supervised by the Colonial Office in London, and it maintained contacts with Husayn through Lawrence, among others. Relations with eastern Arabia, in contrast, were directed by the government of India through various officials in the Gulf. The British at Cairo backed Husayn as the best hope for Arabia. They underestimated Abd al-Aziz's potential in the east and did not appreciate the need to have friends there. Conversely, the British in India, the Gulf, and after World War I in Iraq were aware of Abd al-Aziz's ability and did appreciate that need.[3]

Although Husayn received greater support, including money and weapons, in the end Abd al-Aziz was the stronger. He defeated Hu-

King Abd al-Aziz, 1880–1953 (courtesy of Aramco)

sayn's forces and was proclaimed ruler of the Kingdom of Hijaz in
1926. He was already Sultan of Nejd, to the east. In 1932 these two
areas were joined to form the Kingdom of Saudi Arabia, with outstanding unity and order.

THE LEAN YEARS BEFORE OIL

Before oil was discovered and successfully exploited, Arabia was
a poor land. Although Abd al-Aziz's position improved after unification, he had to struggle to make ends meet. According to Philby's
account in *The Heart of Arabia,* written a decade before Abd al-Aziz
unified the country, he told Philby that all he had in the treasury was
£3,000 and $4,000. The government's yearly receipts totaled what
was then roughly equivalent to $500,000. Charges paid by pilgrims
to Mecca constituted a main source of revenue. There was also the
zakat, or tithe, of one sheep per forty sheep or one goat per five
camels (those with fewer were exempt from the tithe). As to other
revenues in these years, Philby quotes Abd al-Aziz as follows: "Until
quite recently I had regular opportunities of adding to my resources
by the capture of livestock and other booty in expeditions against
recalcitrant tribes, but now God has blessed my territories with peace,
and that source of revenue is lost to me." In 1917 Britain began to
subsidize Abd al-Aziz with £5,000 per month. This practice was sus-
pended in 1924, but subsidies continued irregularly during World War
II. Britain also sent him rifles from time to time.[4]

As worldwide economic conditions improved during the 1920s,
more and more Muslims made the pilgrimage to Mecca, and the government came to expect an average of about 100,000 pilgrims a year.
In 1929 a record number came. Pilgrims commonly brought goods to
sell to cover expenses, and duty paid on these became a mainstay of
revenues. But the revenues of these good years shrank when the onset
of the Great Depression brought a series of lean years. The countries
of the Middle East and Asia, from which most pilgrims came, were
hard hit by falling prices of the raw materials they produced. As a
result, fewer could afford the costly journey to Mecca. In 1930 the
number of pilgrims fell to 80,000 and in 1931 to 40,000; and the
number continued to decline thereafter. Customs receipts fell accord-

ingly. The government was hard put to it to meet the emergency. Taxes were raised and some economies were made.[5]

Abd al-Aziz approached Britain for larger aid, but he would not accept the controls and restrictions Britain required. In 1932, as a last resort, he turned to the Soviet Union, which had recognized his rule in 1926, the first nation to do so, as well as the first to establish a legation (1929) with a Soviet Muslim as the first minister. The experience with Russia was not a happy one. A Soviet ship brought to Jidda a large cargo of goods. But their disposal brought competition with local merchants in Jidda, resulting in a ban on trade with Russia. Later on, in 1932, the Russian representative offered credit on easy terms, including especially needed petroleum products! According to Philby, payment for the goods received may never have been made. Eventually the legation was closed and the personnel ordered home in 1938.[6] Saudi Arabia has since avoided relations with the Russians, whom they deride as "atheistic."

As the effects of the depression lessened, the revenues grew. In 1938 the total was equivalent to about $7 million. The year 1938 also marked the beginning of oil royalties, about $340,000. Meanwhile, the Standard Oil Company of California, the first oil company to operate in Saudi Arabia, tendered some loans to the country through its subsidiary, California Arabian Standard Oil Company, a predecessor of Aramco (see Appendix I, Table 1). At this time about 50 percent of the revenue came from pilgrims and 37 percent from customs.[7] A long drought was ended by welcome rain. But, despite the better outlook, pressure to spend was continuously heavy, and the king and government were in debt to foreign and local interests.[8]

The American government had lagged in recognizing Abd al-Aziz's government, although in 1928 he had proposed recognition. The State Department wanted to wait to see whether American interests were actual or merely potential. Only in 1938 was oil found in commercial quantities. Meanwhile, Russia and Britain elevated consulates to legations at Jidda. United States recognition finally came in 1931, with the minister to Egypt doubling as minister to Saudi Arabia in absentia. According to the record, Bert Fish, American minister to Egypt, was the first to make an official visit to Saudi Arabia. He presented his credentials in February 1940. Not until 1942 did Washington decide to establish a legation at Jidda. James S. Moose, Jr., was named chargé d'affaires and consul; he was named minister resident in 1943. The United States also was slow to raise its legation to the rank of embassy, principally because of the Palestine problem. The posts at Cairo and Baghdad were so raised in 1946; embassy rank was finally established in Saudi Arabia in 1949 with J. Rives Childs becoming the first ambassador.[9]

THE AMERICANS FIND OIL

The history of the search for, and the discovery and development of, oil in the Middle East has been fully told.[10] Here I shall only summarize the early events, particularly as they relate to Saudi Arabia.

There was sporadic exploration for oil in Saudi Arabia before World War I, touched off by the discovery of oil in Iran in 1908. But no productive deposits were found. The start of oil development by American interests in Saudi Arabia resulted from two principal happenings. The first was the visit, in 1931, to Abd al-Aziz of Charles R. Crane, an American philanthropist who had several times been in the Middle East. The second related to the discovery of oil in 1932 on Bahrain Island near the eastern shore of Arabia. (The Saudis refer to the Arabian rather than the Persian Gulf.)

In 1931 Crane, who had helped the imam of Yemen develop resources and communications, offered to donate the services of K. S. Twitchell, an American mining engineer in his employ, to Ibn Saud on the condition that he provide facilities to enable Twitchell to examine the country's resources. The king accepted, and shortly thereafter Twitchell began studying mineral possibilities, which he found were not very promising.[11]

In 1932 the king wanted Twitchell to arrange for American oil geologists and drillers to begin exploration. Also, early in 1932 the Standard Oil Company of California (SOCAL) was drilling on Bahrain. Two years earlier SOCAL had failed to persuade Abd al-Aziz to grant exploration rights on the neighboring Saudi mainland. At this point, Twitchell urged awaiting the results from Bahrain. Exploration was expensive, and he believed that if oil were found there American companies would be interested. After much discussion the king agreed.[12]

When oil was found in commercial quantities on Bahrain in June 1932,[13] the king came under pressure from two sides. The more fanatical leaders of the Wahhabi sect were "reluctant to open his country to the infidel." But the king's finance minister, Shaykh Abd Allah Sulayman, favored development, as did business interests and Philby, who had influence with the king. The king decided in favor of development. Soon after the Bahrain find the king's representatives, Shaykh Abd Allah Sulayman and Shaykh Yusuf Yasin, told Twitchell that the king wanted him to try to find capital for development. Twitchell consulted several leading international oil companies, but some were bound by agreements barring them from entry to Arabia. SOCAL was not so bound; nor was its rival, the Iraq Petroleum Company (IPC), which had American, British, and French participation. Twitchell went to Jidda early in 1933, with Lloyd N. Hamilton of SOCAL, to negotiate.[14]

Negotiations with SOCAL and its competitor took place during the depths of the Great Depression. Abd al-Aziz's financial position was desperate. The much-needed revenue from the yearly pilgrimage to Mecca shrank as economic conditions worsened. The king needed a loan as well as current revenue from a concession. And he needed gold. (At that time, the British gold sovereign, while no longer standard in Britain, was used for larger transactions in Saudi Arabia. Elsewhere in the Middle East and throughout the world gold became much in demand, lawfully or in black or gray markets, for hoarding and/or as currency.)

Prospects for oil in commercial quantities on the mainland were uncertain. At that time little geological work had been done, and no reliable maps existed. Even Abd al-Aziz remained skeptical about prospects up to the time of the discovery in 1938. Thus, when the concession was negotiated, neither the Saudis nor the firms competing for the concession had any idea of what oil if any might be found. No one then dreamed that what may be the world's richest oilfields underlay Saudi Arabia's deserts, with perhaps a third of the world's estimated oil reserves as of 1982.

SOCAL's representative, Lloyd N. Hamilton, had been negotiating for several weeks before IPC representative Stephen H. Longrigg, who was British, arrived. Hamilton had already made a concrete proposal—he had offered a loan and future specified payments, all in gold; asked for a sixty-year concession; and promised to start exploration promptly. Because of the doubt whether there was oil in Saudi Arabia, Longrigg sought only exploring rights. SOCAL's greater willingness to take a chance helped it to win quickly over its rival. But the decisive factor was the offer of a loan and future payments in gold.[15]

Shaykh Abd Allah Sulayman, backed by Abd al-Aziz, was a tough negotiator. The concession agreement was finally concluded on May 29, 1933; it ran for sixty years, covering a large part of eastern Saudi Arabia and entailing preferential rights in other areas. SOCAL agreed to make an immediate loan of 30,000 gold pounds or its equivalent and, after eighteen months, an additional 20,000 gold pounds. Both were recoverable from half of royalties. Rentals of 5,000 gold pounds were payable yearly in advance from the date of the agreement until such time as oil was found in commercial quantities. Then royalties of four shillings gold (i.e., a fifth of a gold pound) or its equivalent became payable per ton of oil produced.[16]

For a time it was uncertain whether gold could be found for payments required by the final agreement. While the negotiations were in progress in Saudi Arabia, President Franklin D. Roosevelt took the United States off the gold standard and declared a bank holiday. Even major companies like SOCAL faced financial difficulties.

To conduct operations SOCAL formed a subsidiary, California Arabian Standard Oil Company (CASOC); in 1944 the name was changed to Arabian American Oil Company, commonly called Aramco. The first geologists arrived without delay, and the first well was spudded on April 20, 1935. The search for oil was arduous, in barren desert that was violently hot for half of the year. Thomas C. Barger, then a young geologist and later head of Aramco, has written to me:

The oil was not easy to find—it took four and a half years of intensive geological work and drilling to come up with Dammam Dome. The fruit of my three years of geological work was a dry hole at Ma'aqalah, at a time when there was no other known prospect save Abu Hadriyah then being drilled.

At last oil was found in large amounts in 1938, at about 4,700 feet. Well "Lucky Seven" was brought in by SOCAL's chief geologist, Max Steinecke, after six disappointments. A sea outlet was built, and when the first tanker was loaded in May 1939, Abd al-Aziz was happy to open the valve of the loading line.[17]

In 1939, on the eve of World War II, SOCAL was granted rights in expanded areas (comprising an area about as large as California and Oregon combined) with the best prospects for oil, by a supplemental agreement for a sixty-year period. Abd al-Aziz granted these rights despite competition from British and Japanese bidders, who offered more money for rights to smaller areas. The king believed that the latter were acting jointly to seek concessions for German and Italian interests, whose countries he suspected of territorial ambitions. SOCAL made a cash payment of $1.2 million in gold and agreed to an annual rental of $170,000 until oil was found in sufficient amounts for commercial exploitation. Minister Fish reported from Egypt that the king said he had "faith in the United States and is satisfied with and trusts the California company."[18]

When World War II began in the fall of 1939, shortly after the second concession was granted, eight producing wells had been completed. Wartime conditions interfered with flow of supplies and shipments to markets, and production could not be greatly increased. Foreign staff was cut by about two thirds in two years. Nevertheless, geological exploration and mapping continued with promising results. The company drilled many water wells, which pleased the government and the people. Shortly before the war's end a refinery with capacity of 50,000 barrels per day was built at Ra's Tannurah, and it went on stream in September 1945.[19]

2

WORLD WAR II:
SAUDI ARABIA NEEDS HELP

Saudi Arabia's vast wealth today makes it difficult to realize how hard it was for Abd al-Aziz to make ends meet during the war. He had to implore the United States and Britain to help.

WARTIME STRINGENCY

When World War II broke out in 1939, rapid growth of revenue from oil seemed assured. From its modest beginning of $340,000 in 1938 it grew to $3.21 million in 1939 and to $4.79 million in 1940 (including Aramco advances). Then wartime conditions restricted increase of oil production and export. Worse was to come in 1940 when overseas pilgrimage was banned by Britain after Italy, which controlled Ethiopia, entered the war.[1] Customs revenue dropped, both from loss of duty paid by pilgrims and because wartime disruption caused imports to fall off. Loss of import of cereals was especially serious because Saudi Arabia was not self-sufficient in food. The government's revenues, apart from oil, dropped from the equivalent of $7 million in 1938 to about $2 million by 1941. Including the moderate revenue from oil and advances by SOCAL, total receipts during the years 1941–43 averaged only about $5.5 million yearly. (Details of the available data, including oil revenues, are shown in Appendix I, Table 2.)

King Abd al-Aziz could not run his government on $5.5 million yearly. Desperate for aid, he turned to Britain, SOCAL, and the United States. Britain began giving Abd al-Aziz £400,000 (then about $1.6 million) yearly. As the king's income shrank the aid increased, and during 1943–44 total British aid equaled about $37 million.[2] Abd al-Aziz also repeatedly pressed SOCAL for advances against royalties, and the company felt bound to comply. As of early 1943 advances totaled about $10 million, and a further $2 million was advanced in 1944.[3]

Various plans were considered by the United States government from 1941 to 1944 to provide Abd al-Aziz with more financial aid. One such plan, presented to Roosevelt by SOCAL's president, James A. Moffett, in 1943, would have involved funneling monies to the king by means of guaranteed purchases of CASOC oil by the United States government. That was not found practicable. Another plan, put forward in 1943 and strongly backed by Interior Secretary Harold L. Ickes and Navy Secretary Frank Knox, would have entailed total or partial takeover of CASOC by the United States government, which would make advances to the king.[4] That idea met strong opposition in the State Department, and Alexander Kirk, Fish's successor as minister to Saudi Arabia, telegraphed that it would "tend to tar us with the same brush" as the imperialists.[5] The scheme was dropped because of widespread objection when it became publicly known, including protests by other oil companies of possible government competition.* Early in 1944 SOCAL announced that it would build a privately owned and financed refinery in Saudi Arabia. It also went ahead with plans for the trans-Arabia pipeline to the Mediterranean (Tapline).

---

*American strategic interest in foreign oil came sharply to the fore after the United States joined the war December 7, 1941. The United States was changing from a net exporter to an importer of oil. For a full discussion of this episode see Anderson, *Aramco, the United States and Saudi Arabia* (Princeton, N.J.: Princeton University Press, 1981), pp. 42–67.

The need for some form of adequate financial aid was quite real. Kirk urged direct financial aid as early as 1941, stating that failure to act would be "a disregard of realities." But the United States, with its strict laws and the cumbersome procedures of Congress, could not easily make a loan. At length, early in 1943 Roosevelt declared Saudi Arabia eligible for lend-lease aid, holding that its defense was vital to the defense of the United States.[6] This declaration opened a way for direct American aid.

Some aid was provided by sending cereals.[7] But larger American aid could be provided in silver and gold, taking advantage of the lend-lease law and laws concerning silver. This suited Saudi Arabia because it supplied money usable upon receipt. The full-weight silver riyal, similar to the Indian rupee, was the coin most widely used. To speed delivery minting was done in India and England, swapping silver in the United States for silver there. A total of 22,747,431 ounces of silver for coinage was supplied to June 30, 1946.[8] To meet the need for gold, the United States provided $1 million worth of gold bars of 5 ounces and up in 1944; and in 1945 it sent $1 million worth of gold discs worth $20.00 each. In 1947–48, $2 million of discs equal in weight and fineness to the British gold sovereign were provided. The sovereign contains 7.23238 grams (0.23542 oz.) of fine gold, equivalent to $8.24 at the then parity of $35.00 per fine ounce. But after Britain left the gold standard in 1931 the sovereign brought a premium price, which in Saudi Arabia rose as high as $24.00 during the war. The public readily absorbed the gold. Prices realized from it in Saudi Arabia are not available, but doubtless the discs realized somewhat less than the British sovereign.[9]

These forms of aid were slow, however, and Abd al-Aziz wanted a loan for urgent needs. In 1944 Saudi Arabia received only $1.66 million from oil, augmented by Aramco's advancing $2 million. On December 22, 1944, Secretary of State Cordell Hull sent to President Roosevelt a proposal for aid. Lend-lease aid was proving helpful but could be only temporary; hence aid should be sought via legislation and loans by the Export-Import Bank. The president approved Hull's proposals.[10]

The State Department pressed for action, but the ways of Congress seemed endless. Fear, probably exaggerated, was expressed that lacking American aid the oil concession with its huge potential might be lost. After the war ended in September Foreign Minister Faysal ibn Abd al-Aziz, who later became king, was told that the Export-Import Bank would lend Saudi Arabia $5 million.[11]

BRITAIN'S SPHERE OF INFLUENCE AND THE UNITED STATES

Beginning in 1941 proposals for American aid to Saudi Arabia raised issues not only of how the United States and Britain should share in providing aid but of their respective responsibilities and stakes in Saudi Arabia and the Middle East. Each country put forward proposals to improve the financial situation. All these issues were intermingled in the discussions that took place.

The United States was a newcomer in a region where Britain had long exercised power. When the question of American aid first came before President Roosevelt in July 1941, he wrote to Jesse Jones of the Reconstruction Finance Corporation: "Will you tell the British I hope that they can take care of the king of Saudi Arabia. This is a little far afield for us." Minister Kirk thought this unwise: the king was firmly independent and should not be given the impression that the United States identified his kingdom with the British system of spheres of influence, colonies, protectorates, and mandates. He gave the king an equivocal answer.[12] During these years the two countries often sought to cooperate, but in fact they became rivals.

Both countries, from their differing perspectives on the situation, made earnest and repeated efforts looking toward creating a sound and workable monetary system in Saudi Arabia. Giving aid was difficult because the unrelated silver and gold coins were fluctuating in wartime even more erratically than in time of peace. Shortages of riyals were reported. As a solution, the British proposed a Saudi Arabia Currency Control Board in London, composed of the Saudi minister and two men from the Bank of England. Such boards managed the currencies of colonies and countries in which Britain had a special interest. Britain would provide sterling to secure notes issued in Saudi Arabia.[13]

This plan met strong objection in the State Department where officials believed that the by now already large United States interest in

Saudi Arabia justified having a say in such matters. Also, the oil company expressed concern. So the Treasury sent John W. Gunter to Saudi Arabia to investigate. Chargé Moose was instructed to "assure" the Saudi Arabian government that no such plan was adopted until Gunter could see the king. Meanwhile, Washington proposed to the British that the two countries work together for a "sound long-range currency system."[14]

Repeatedly during the war the Americans and British discussed sending a financial adviser. This was mentioned several times to both King Abd al-Aziz and Foreign Minister Faysal, but neither took action.[15] The British proposed offering the services of an Indian Sunni Muslim, whose loyalties of course could be expected to lie with the British. Ambassador John G. Winant telegraphed from London in July 1944, apparently reflecting British views: "A Christian financial adviser will certainly find difficulties, in obtaining information and in getting his advice accepted, which will not apply to the same extent to a Moslem."[16] But the idea of sending this expert was dropped. Also, help in creating a central bank, either by the United States alone or jointly with Britain, was discussed several times.[17]

Despite all the talk, it is significant that no real action about financial reforms took place until well after the war. Abd al-Aziz appeared to sit out the American-British rivalry during the war years, but it is true that he was taking the significant step of generally tending to favor the United States.

Toward the war's end, in February 1945, Abd al-Aziz and Roosevelt met on the American cruiser *Quincy*, on Great Bitter Lake in the Suez Canal. Roosevelt was returning from the conference at Yalta with Churchill and Stalin. The king was taken to the *Quincy* from Jidda on the American destroyer *Murphy*. The two men were able to quickly establish a very friendly relationship. The king told an associate that meeting Roosevelt was "the high point of my entire life." And according to Minister Eddy, who interpreted for their talk, the king said the two were "twin" brothers in age, as chiefs of state and in physical disability. Roosevelt called the king "fortunate to still have the use of your legs." Abd al-Aziz replied that his "legs grow feebler every year." Roosevelt gave him a wheelchair. They talked of a wide range of problems including the favorable state of the war and the responsibilities of governing. Also, they talked of the problem of Palestine, as to which the president gave what were taken as gratifying assurances. They also discussed Saudi–British–American relations. Abd al-Aziz said he liked the English, but Eddy quoted him as saying they tell him that ''they seek a priority for Britain in Saudi Arabia'', and that ''Saudi Arabia lies in a path bounded with sterling controls, connected by British communications . . . defended by the Royal Navy and Army,'' and that ''America's political interest in Saudi Arabia is a transitory war-interest.'' This line of talk apparently reflected the views of Minister Jordan.

The arrangements for the meeting also brought into sharp focus how Abd al-Aziz's way of life differed from that of the modern world. An account in the *Los Angeles Times* of June 11, 1974, by William J. Coughlin tells this story. The king, he wrote, arrived at Jidda to board the *Murphy* with a retinue of 200 including some women of the *hareem*. The captain had wanted to take only the king and a dozen others, but finally the party was cut to 48 men. They spread rugs on the *Murphy*'s deck and erected a royal tent. A *dhow,* besides bringing water from Mecca for the king, pulled alongside with 86 sheep—the king could eat meat only from sheep killed on board. Finally the captain compromised on taking 10 sheep.

Three days after the meeting Abd al-Aziz went on by road to Fayum in Egypt to meet Prime Minister Winston Churchill. Eddy, on the basis of a talk with Abd al-Aziz, reported that the king and Churchill differed widely on the problem of Palestine, about which they argued vigorously. Not surprisingly, the king did not warm up to Churchill as he did to Roosevelt, who appeared sympathetic to the Arab viewpoint. Eddy quoted his adverse reaction: ''The contrast between the President and Mr. Churchill is very great. Mr. Churchill speaks deviously, evades understanding, changes the subject to avoid commitment. . . . The President seeks understanding.''[18]

Churchill, writing about his meeting with Abd al-Aziz, made no comment on the substance of matters discussed. But he had been told that neither alcoholic beverages nor smoking were allowed in the royal presence. When hosting a luncheon for the king, he said to the interpreter that if it was the king's religion ''to deprive himself'' of these, he must point out that his ''rule of life prescribed as an absolutely sacred rite smoking cigars and also the drinking of alcohol before, after, and if need be during all meals and in the intervals between them.'' Abd al-Aziz, he said, "graciously accepted the position" and offered him a delicious glass of water from Mecca's sacred well.[19]

Eddy reported in September 1945 that Abd al-Aziz was going to continue to "sit out" American-British rivalry. Nonetheless, Roosevelt's forecast, at the meeting on the *U.S.S. Quincy* that after the war he "would envisage a decline of spheres of influence in favor of the Open Door," proved entirely correct.[20] Britain had suffered deeply and grievously from the war, and the Labor government that took over in July 1945 sought in a very straightforward way to disengage from imperialism. Foreign Secretary Ernest Bevin said that Britain wished "to leave behind for ever the idea of one country dominating another."

This set the stage for future development, and a major turning point as to American and British responsibility in the Middle East came early in 1947, when Britain asked the United States to take over financial and military support for Greece and Turkey to help to resist Soviet pressure. Prompt American acceptance was embodied in the Truman Doctrine. From then onward the United States began to take on increasing and preponderant responsibility for security in the eastern Mediterranean and West Asia.

With Saudi Arabia's growing stake in oil after World War II American influence grew, not only in the oil area, but in the business center in Jidda. Ambassador Childs reported in June 1950 "widespread UK dissatisfaction with subordinate role in Saudi Arabia which it forced to take increasingly over past few years." But the view in at least some quarters in London was different. American Ambassador Lewis W. Douglas reported in July that "responsible Foreign Office officials" recognized the importance of the American presence and of cooperation between the two nations as a stabilizing factor in a troubled area.[21] When I arrived in Saudi Arabia in 1951, I was to find British officials and the business community friendly and cooperative.

3

OLD STRUCTURES, GROWING PROBLEMS

With new wealth from oil in prospect, problems that had failed of solution during the war remained in 1945. How manage the receiving of the flow of foreign currency, mostly dollars? How control and allocate the spending? The traditional structure of government, the economy, currency, and financial institutions could not cope with the new situation. The need for reforms became more and more clear.

King Abd al-Aziz wanted to modernize. Some advisers such as Shaykh Abd Allah Sulayman gave support, but others saw modernization as Satan's work. At first, religious conservatives broke mirrors and human portraits and rejected the radio. As to the latter, however, the king had a clinching argument: the Koran's sacred words could be broadcast over the air.

A master in internal politics, the king lacked experience with complicated financial affairs and with administration. Despite the restraining influence of his finance minister, King Abd al-Aziz's generosity led to spending without effective control.

NEW WEALTH FROM OIL

The war's ending cleared the way for a gushing flow of oil, along with a gushing flow of royalties. Aramco could have access to supplies, and markets could expand rapidly. Meanwhile, its experts had mapped and explored and were ready to drill new wells. Late in the war it was able to get enough materials to build a refinery to handle 50,000 barrels daily; expansion to 150,000 barrels per day was soon begun.*

The Tapline, 1,068 miles from the oil-producing eastern region of Saudi Arabia to Sidon on the Mediterranean Sea, was begun in 1947. Construction of Tapline called for difficult negotiations for the right to cross Jordan, Syria, and Lebanon. It was a major project, mostly over desert with sandy, rocky, and often irregular terrain. The first tanker was loaded at Sidon in December 1950. Tapline saved Suez Canal dues and avoided a trip of many thousands of miles to European markets. Thus, its $240 million cost was justified.

Also in 1947, at the behest of the U.S. State Department, Aramco began construction of a 345-mile railroad from the oil part of Dammam to Riyadh—Abd al-Aziz had wanted such a rail line for some time—and the line was opened in 1951. The cost was $52.5 million, to be repaid by deductions from royalties.

Aramco's expansion brought about a corresponding growth of oil revenue. This ended Saudi Arabia's need for foreign financial aid, which Washington had overestimated at $43 million over five years from 1945.[1] Payments by Aramco grew from only $3 million to $5 million during the war, but rose to $10.4 million in 1946 and to $56.7 million in 1950 (see Appendix I, Table 1).

Yet the government was not satisfied with its share. Finance Minister Abd Allah Sulayman was under continual pressure from the king and his court to provide more money, and during most of 1950 the minister pressed Aramco hard for larger payments. Aramco resisted, believing that giving in would bring only more demands. The company argued that larger payments would hurt it in marketing oil in

*SOCAL broadened its base when it took in The Texas Company, now Texaco, in 1936, and arranged in 1948 to be owned 30 percent each by SOCAL, The Texas Company, and Standard Oil Company (New Jersey), now Exxon, with Socony-Vacuum Oil Company, now Mobil, owning 10 percent.

competition with other producers. The government retorted that Aramco was making big money and could afford to pay. The company had, after all, recouped its investment in five years.

Talks became bitter, and ultimatums were issued by the government. Ambassador Childs wondered whether a showdown might be desirable. He felt that the government's new wealth was leading to "prodigality and improvidence." Washington believed that negotiated changes would be in the interest of both parties. The upshot was a conciliatory message to Foreign Minister Prince Faysal ibn Abd al-Aziz. The message pointed out that Aramco had performed extraordinarily well, that its ability to pay was not unlimited, and that the mutual interest of the company and Saudi Arabia argued for moderation and cooperation.[2]

Saudi Arabia wanted to add an income tax to royalties, thereby receiving more than a 50/50 split of profits. The government engaged an American tax expert who drafted a decree to this effect (dated November 4, 1950). The decree was then issued by the king, although no agreement had been reached with Aramco. The 50/50 arrangement was already the rule in Venezuela, and the company refused to compromise on this point. Intense negotiations continued. Finally an amending decree was issued as of December 27. A detailed agreement covering its application to the company was signed on December 30 and took effect on January 1, 1951. It provided that the total of all taxes, royalties, rentals, and exactions by the government should not in any year exceed half of Aramco's gross income after deducting operating costs, including depreciation and taxes payable to any foreign country. Aramco was given the option to pay in the currencies of Saudi Arabia or other currencies in the proportions received from sales.[3]

The agreement greatly increased the government's revenue. In 1951 oil production was 39 percent greater than in 1950. But revenue nearly doubled—from $56.7 million to $110.0 million (see Appendix I, Tables 1 and 3).

SPENDING VERSUS RESTRAINT

When oil production and revenue burgeoned after the war, spending grew even faster. The king and his government, released at last from the crushing poverty of centuries, could not wait for the expected oil bonanza. The Export-Import Bank's loan of $5 million for public works and development, concluded just after the war, now seemed insufficient. The bank proposed a further loan of $10 million, with control of use of the money, which Abd al-Aziz rejected.* Finally in August 1946 an agreement was signed. Aramco would repay the $10 million loan from oil royalties. (To get around the problem of interest, which is contrary to Islamic law, the series of payments would total somewhat more than principal.)[4]

Governments, like individuals, have the urge to spend more whenever income suddenly increases. It was quickly forgotten that up till 1939 the government had managed with revenues equal to about $7 million yearly. One might have hoped that income of many tens of millions of dollars would produce a surplus for development and reserve. In this case, however, Parkinson's law did not mean merely that spending rose to the level of income. Rather, it rose to income plus borrowing.

King Abd al-Aziz, besides lacking the background to deal with this kind of issue, was in weakening health. His long struggles to build his country made him pay a price. He died in 1953. Immediate priorities for him were to aid the tribes to subsist as best they could in their barren desert life, to reward those who helped him, and to look after the welfare of his numerous retainers. His strong wish to modernize led to his approving projects he believed to be in his country's interests, without sufficiently weighing their cost. He never lived lavishly, but as the money came in, he did not worry about others maintaining costly establishments. It took some time to cut the coat according to the cloth. Spending beyond income, and various excesses in spending, were not finally brought under control until Prince Faysal's reforms of the late 1950s, by which time he was heir apparent.

Treating the state treasury as the king's purse had been common practice even into modern times in Europe. Similar practices have persisted in many countries, including Communist states where some in authority are more equal than others—even in the United States,

---

*The bank made a further loan of $15 million in 1950, also for public works and development, to be repaid over ten years (FRUS 1950 V, pp. 1180–84).

Congress has often granted valuable perquisites to its members (usually by voice vote).

Finance Minister Abd Allah Sulayman had his problems. In 1947 he prepared a budget reducing some of the outlay. But it was a complete failure, since the king vetoed some cuts and also called for funds outside the budget. By 1949 oil revenue was $39 million, yet in December the financial crisis was so serious that the government had difficulty in meeting its obligations and postponed various development projects that had been previously approved.

Finally there were signs of realizing that something had to be done. In February 1950 Ambassador Childs reported a talk with the heir apparent, Prince Saud ibn Abd al-Aziz, who was worried about the "deplorable state" of the finances. He saw the need for "thoroughgoing reforms" and said that when he came to power he "would spare no one in taking necessary measures."[5] (Unfortunately, after becoming king he did not give effect to these ideas.)

In November 1950 Childs's successor, Ambassador Raymond A. Hare, while conversing with the king's close adviser, Yusuf Yasin, made a comparison that, when repeated to the monarch, caught his imagination: "It would be a poor way to correct the continual loss of water merely by pouring in more water and not fixing the wasteful leak." At last the king was ready to have a budget and professional assistance.[6]

FOREIGN ADVISERS: FROM TALK TO REALITY

In a world where operations of government were becoming more and more complicated, few Saudi Arabians were yet qualified to cope with the new problems that resulted from the oil bonanza and its consequences. Hardly any had had either experience in the complexities of public administration or adequate understanding of economic problems. Prince Faysal stood out as the foreign minister, not only because he had outstanding character and ability, but because he had much foreign experience too. Finance Minister Abd Allah Sulayman as a young man had business experience in India. But his native ability and shrewdness were more valuable. Very few Saudis had trained abroad, and to man the government it was necessary to rely heavily on men recruited from nearby Arab countries. Notable among these in finance was the Lebanese Najib Bey Salihah, an articulate person whose ability was to lead him to become assistant deputy minister of finance.

As mentioned in Chapter 2, no significant progress toward providing expert aid in financial reform materialized during World War II.[7] After the war ended a variety of plans were put forward, including one, in 1947, by two vice-presidents of Guaranty Trust Company of New York (now the Morgan Guaranty Trust Company of New York), which helped the country to manage oil revenue received in dollars and also made loans against future royalties. These experts proposed a currency reform to be handled by a joint international commission. There was also a French-sponsored plan for such a commission. Nothing came of these proposals.

In the spring of 1948 Judd Polk, U.S. Treasury Department representative in Cairo, visited Saudi Arabia and found serious monetary problems. Rates varied widely between sovereigns and riyals, and the values of both varied with respect to foreign currencies (see Appendix I, Table 4). In early 1948 the sovereign had fallen from $16 in January to $13 in May; the riyal, from 68.00 to 61.45 per sovereign. (The lows in that year were $12.75 and 52.25 respectively.) The government, failing to link the two at 65.00, reduced the rate to 62.00.

Polk pointed out that a link was not workable. In place of the full-weight silver riyal, he favored a token coin with less silver and, eventually, a well-secured paper currency.* He hoped that one or more foreign consultants could come to advise on the situation. Washington concurred with him that a riyal-sovereign link would fail and that Saudi Arabia "should not rush into new currency plan without careful study and preparation." Polk also recommended improving the government's accounting and statistics and advocated creation of a central bank, beginning with a "Government Financial Agency" to handle the government's receipts and payments and to stabilize foreign exchange rates. He further stressed the basic problem of how in a "barren land" oil revenue, a depletable asset, could be converted "into lasting productive gains."[8]

---

*Saudi Arabians distrusted paper currency, and this distrust was to remain a problem for some time.

The erratic monetary situation caused difficulties for Aramco, Saudi Arabia's biggest enterprise. Royalties were due in sovereigns, but in March 1948 the company arranged to have the option of paying dollars at $12 per sovereign.[9] For payrolls the company needed both sovereigns and riyals, which were difficult to obtain at reasonable rates. Saudi Arabia was only a small factor in the worldwide market for sovereigns, and the supply of riyals in large amounts was uncertain—their value was affected by the price of silver abroad.

During 1948 Aramco's officials periodically discussed the problems with the State and Treasury departments. In October the company's financial vice-president proposed that George Eddy of the Treasury's Office of International Finance go with him to Saudi Arabia to take part in discussing the situation and for possible action. Saudi Arabia had not formally asked for American advice, but high officials had several times indicated that they would welcome it.[10]

As a result of the discussions in Washington, Eddy and Raymond F. Mikesell of the State Department went to Saudi Arabia to be available to give informal technical advice on monetary problems. They traveled independently, not with Aramco personnel, and they acted as individuals, not as official representatives.[11]

In talks with Saudi officials they pointed out that to link the sovereign and riyal was impossible because rates depended on factors outside the country's control. They urged abandoning the attempt to set a rate of 62–1, which was failing, and they urged abandoning efforts to control foreign exchange transactions, a policy that obstructed trade and could not be made to work well. They proposed that the riyal be the basic currency and linked to the dollar at 4–1; the government should stand ready to buy riyals at 25.25 cents and sell at 25. To support the plan, they proposed a stabilization fund of $10 million in New York, to be gradually increased by part of oil royalties.[12] They also made a number of other important technical recommendations, the most important having to do with the relation of the full-weight riyals to the price of silver in the world market and how the value of the full-weight riyal could be affected by fluctuations in the market.

Their plan was put into effect and succeeded for several months. But it failed in the spring of 1949 when shipments of 60 million riyals coined abroad began to arrive; the total coined to that time was about 100 million (see Appendix I, Table 5).[13] Putting this large number of new riyals in circulation was inflationary and promptly caused their value to fall. In addition, lower exchange rates made it profitable to smuggle them out because of their full-weight silver content. There was strong suspicion of profiteering connected with the excessive ordering.

Other plans were forthcoming. In response to a request from the Saudi government, the British Treasury sent a representative in early 1949 to discuss currency reform, and he made new recommendations. He proposed a unit like the Iraqi dinar, equal in value to the pound sterling, to which it would be linked. He revived the proposal of a joint British–Saudi Arabian Currency Board, which had been rejected during the war. In 1950 Paul Parker, U.S. Treasury representative in the Middle East, proposed stabilizing the riyal as the basic unit and relating it to a new Saudi gold sovereign. Nothing came of these plans.

The next project to appear was the idea of Christian Delaby, manager of the French Banque de l'Indochine in Jidda, whose advice Saudi officials had first sought in 1948. He persuaded the government to mint in Paris 2 million Saudi gold sovereigns, a new coin equal in weight and fineness to the British sovereign, and to link the riyal to the new gold coin, probably at 40–1. He thought of holding the riyal at about 26 to 27 cents, which early in 1951 was a little below its value at the world silver price. If riyals were smuggled out, they would be replaced by new coinage until, he hoped, a token riyal containing less silver could be issued. The new gold coin at 40–1 would thus have a value of $10.40 to $10.80, compared with about $12.00 for the British sovereign at that time. The manager of the Banque de l'Indochine at Jidda, M. Robert, who succeeded Delaby, was to control issuing riyals in connection with putting out the new gold coins.

Saudi officials ordered the new gold sovereigns but, after having done so, became puzzled as to what to do about Delaby's proposals. There was doubt as to whether Saudi Arabia, with its undeveloped financial structure, could operate any such plan successfully. And changes in the world values of silver and gold could make such a plan unworkable.

Meanwhile, the inconvenience and costs of erratically changing monetary conditions continued. The government found it unsatisfactory to have to rely upon foreign banks to manage its rapidly growing revenue, which was mostly in foreign currencies and had to be converted into riyals and/or sovereigns as needed. Aramco found it hard to get the kinds of money needed for operations, and smaller businesses and the public were similarly troubled.

All the proposals and comings and goings of experts came to naught until December 1950. But finally the time was ripe, and King Abd al-Aziz was ready for action. It was natural for him at this time to turn to the United States. Aramco had justified his initial confidence by performing excellently. And his confidence in the United States had been reinforced by his visit with Roosevelt in 1945 (Chapter 2). The confidence survived, although with difficulty, the rift in policy toward Israel.

Ambassador Hare reported that Saudi Arabia asked for five American experts: one for currency and coinage matters and two each for accounting procedures and customs organization. The State Department proceeded to implement this request and made it clear that the experts would be sent only as advisers, to make recommendations but not to act as administrators of these recommendations.[14]

4

APPROACH TO
REFORMS

In 1951 there seemed to be a good prospect of devising appropriately improved financial machinery and procedures for Saudi Arabia, and of persuading King Abd al-Aziz and his government to accept them. The possibility of finding ways to reform the currency system were less good because of the uncertainty about the future values of silver and gold. In contrast to most financially troubled countries, there was no lack of revenues. But spending was out of control, and only sad experience could curb this.

BEGINNING OF A MISSION

Early in 1951 I had a call from Washington asking if I would be interested in going to Saudi Arabia. The State and Treasury departments were making arrangements for the financial mission requested by Abd al-Aziz. I learned later that George Luthringer of the International Monetary Fund had suggested that I head the mission. Saudi monetary problems centered on silver, gold, and foreign exchange, and George knew of my long experience in dealing with such problems as financial adviser in China. Intrigued by the idea of being a sort of financial Lawrence of Arabia, I said I would go.

It was a rare privilege to be called upon to take part in helping two very different countries that, after moving actively for unification, were anxious to lay suitable financial foundations. In China during the 1920s and 1930s, where I became financial adviser in 1929, Chiang Kai-shek was putting down the warlords and giving effect to Sun Yat-sen's dream of a unified, strong, and progessing nation. (Despite Japanese interference and Communist opposition, China's Nationalists had outstanding success until Japanese moves led to all-out war in 1937.) Meanwhile, also beginning in the 1920s, Abd al-Aziz was unifying Arabia's tribes and striving to build an advancing nation. Unification had been well accomplished by 1951 when I was invited to help. But the need remained for fundamental constructive action in the field of finance.

In Washington it did not prove easy to get the mission under way. The United States government had offered to pay the salaries of the mission under the new aid program. This was then generally called Point Four because, as the fourth point in President Truman's inaugural address to Congress in 1949, it had been favorably received and enacted into law. I quickly found that I had to pass through a recently created bureaucratic jungle in Washington. By 1950 the McCarthy era had begun, and every appointee to a sensitive post had to be cleared by the FBI to make certain that he was not a Communist. Since the FBI had a large backlog, such investigations took months.

But Saudi Arabia wanted the mission at once. The solution was to give me a "spot check." In being cleared I was doubtless aided by being known by Secretary of State Dean Acheson and others in the Department of State, as well as by my former connection with Nationalist China. So the Department of State recommended me to the Saudi Arabian government (SAG in the official jargon of those days). The department asked SAG whether it would pay my salary and expenses until I could be transferred to the American rolls. SAG

promptly agreed. On May 28 I signed an agreement with SAG's ambassador in Washington, Asad al-Faqih. I was careful to specify an
air-conditioned house. All these things took three months.

I improved the time by being briefed and by studying books and
documents on Saudi Arabia and the Middle East. Aramco's New York
office was most helpful. Its officers gave me useful documents bearing on the problems with which I would deal. Also, I talked with
officers of Guaranty Trust Company, agent of the Netherlands Trading Society's Jidda branch that handled much of the government's
exchange transactions. Since silver loomed large in currency problems, I talked with officers of Handy and Harman, leading silver
dealers, whose yearly reviews of the silver market have long been
authoritative.

Security checks delayed finding the experts on customs administration, tariff, budget, and public accounting to complete the mission's
staffing. I helped in the search but had to leave before any were
engaged. Eventually, the mission was staffed with John A. Dunaway,
former financial adviser to Liberia, as senior expert to deal with customs administration; Robert B. Kennedy, formerly with the American
Tariff Commission, as tariff expert; and John A. Stacy on budget.
The accounting expert, John Bode, arrived only after my departure
from Saudi Arabia, when Dunaway became head of the group.

En route to Saudi Arabia we were delayed in Cairo because our
house in Jidda was not ready. In Cairo I could be briefed further on
Saudi Arabia and the Middle East situation. That was during the last
days of King Faruq, before the revolution of 1952 headed by Jamal
Abd al-Nasir. We sensed the growing nationalism and desire for
change. The next stage was to fly to Jidda by the British company,
Aden Airways. The DC-3 plane was due to leave at 1:00 A.M. and to
reach Jidda about daylight. But after repeated delays owing to mechanical trouble, during which the passengers were taken to a Cairo
hotel for a couple of hours sleep and breakfast, we took off about
9:00 A.M. The delay at least let us view the desert by daylight.

When I disembarked at the Jidda airport at 2:00 P.M., the July heat
was like a Turkish bath—113 degrees and humid. Ambassador Raymond A. Hare and SAG officials met the plane, and I was taken to

the air-conditioned house assigned as my quarters. Mrs. Young, who had been delayed in Cairo by illness, soon joined me.

THE SETTING, 1951

Jidda had long been the chief port on the Red Sea and the country's main economic center. Diplomatic missions were there rather than in Riyadh. Because of extreme heat and lack of amenities Jidda was considered one of the least desirable posts in the foreign service. When serving as consul in 1923, Reader Bullard had responded as follows to London's inquiry as to what foreign institutions were in Jidda: "There are two foreign institutions in Jidda: a bank, which is closed, and a cemetery, which is open."[1] By 1951 electricity, an ice plant, and an improved water supply had been provided. But most of the city, since enormously expanded and modernized, was then little changed from earlier years.[2] Jidda has been the gateway through

Jidda in 1955 showing the old port (courtesy of Aramco)

which most pilgrims come to the holy city of Mecca, about forty miles inland. According to tradition, Abraham and his son Ishmael laid at Mecca the foundation of the Kaaba, the sacred shrine. On the road from Jidda, as one approached the low hills behind which lies Mecca, there was a sign reading: "Restricted Area, Muslims only permitted." During the pilgrimage season thousands of sheep and goats were seen being herded to Mecca for sacrifice. A devoted Muslim should make a pilgrimage to Mecca if at all possible. In the 1950s about 200,000 came yearly from all over the Muslim world stretching from the Atlantic to the Philippines.

Many paid their expenses by bringing goods to sell. Most came by sea, and others across the desert. But more and more were coming by plane, the modern flying carpet, as an airport adequate for the time had been built. Some pilgrims believe that by walking the hot road from Jidda to Mecca they may gain extra credit in heaven. Pilgrim dues were a financial mainstay of the government before the era of oil, but Abd al-Aziz abolished them in 1952. Much earlier, when he took over power in the region, he put an end to abuses whereby "guides" and desert tribes often robbed or otherwise preyed upon pilgrims. It was interesting to visit the port and see the pilgrims disembark en route to Mecca, many carrying bundles of goods to sell.

In 1951 Jidda had perhaps 60,000 people. Old and often ornate buildings several stories high were a main feature, many facing the lagoon. High ceilings and thick walls made from coral blocks mined along the coast had a cooling effect in the trying climate. Often, beds were outside on flat roofs, and some hotels rented outdoor beds.

Ancient narrow streets were common. The *suq,* or market, was a streetlike area covered by rusting sheet metal. Stalls with a great variety of goods lined both sides of the *suq*. Toward the port area, and conveniently near the *suq,* was the building serving as headquarters to receive and clear pilgrims bound for Mecca. In the city's center was a large square where camels and donkeys gathered.

The Jidda of those days had no central water system, and there were hydrants in the square from which donky-drawn two-wheeled tank carts drew water to sell to housewives. Jidda's water came mainly from springs in Wadi Fatimah, an attractive oasis with sunken date gardens about thirty-five miles away in the desert. Also, there were

Aramco's first office in Jidda, 1933 (courtesy of Aramco)

Center of Jidda, 1952 (taken by the author)

Modern Jidda (*courtesy of Aramco*)

wells and a plant to make potable water from seawater. Long ago the climate must have been more hospitable than it is now. When flying over the desert one saw remains of old dams and evidences of irrigation works and ancient settlements. Up to 1952, little archaeological work had been done on them.

The dominating desert was fascinating. From our house we often saw camel trains coming and going. While walking on the desert or seashore late in the day, we looked for the "green flash," which can be seen for a second or two in usually clear weather at the moment when the sun sinks below the horizon. In the traditional Semitic way when the sun set, it was always the twelfth hour or 6:00 P.M. (by European reckoning). Watches and clocks had to be adjusted accordingly when they departed too far from that norm.

Twice in Jidda we were surprised by eclipses. A partial eclipse of the moon began to develop one evening when we were walking on the desert in bright moonlight before bedtime. On a morning sometime later there was an almost total eclipse of the sun, which caused some commotion in the neighborhood. For a people who practically invented astronomy there could be no advance notice since newspapers did not publish the expected dates. Philby tells of once mentioning to Abd al-Aziz the date when Ramadan was to begin. The king rebuked him: "only Allah knows," a well-justified remark in that one must actually sight the new moon and whether or not that can be done on a particular night is unfathomable. A common expression is *in sha' Allah* (Allah willing). It qualified plans and engagements and can mean "wait and see," or "perhaps," or "yes," or "no."

Most people in Saudi Arabia adhere to the fundamentalist Sunnite branch of Islam, although there are Shiites in some areas. Friday is the Muslim Sabbath and generally a day of rest. The Islamic year dates from Muhammad's *hijrah* (emigration or flight) from Mecca to Medina in A.D. 622. Being the lunar year, it is shorter by eleven days than the Gregorian year. Thus, we were in Saudi Arabia in 1371–72. The ninth month, Ramadan, is holy—a period of abstaining from food, drink, and sexual relations from dawn to dusk. This causes real hardship, especially in the summer as it did during our stay. During Ramadan the day begins as soon as white and black threads can be distinguished. Late in the day people wait anxiously to hear the cannon signaling the day's close. As the days pass they look to see the new moon, whose sight marks Ramadan's end.

The people are predominantly the brown Mediterranean type, but there is a strong admixture of black blood. Many slaves have been brought from nearby Africa, and domestic slavery still existed in 1951–52, although with generally kind treatment. The society was male-dominated. Men and women did not mix socially outside the home. In public, women wore long black veils reaching to their ankles. But young girls were unveiled up to the age of puberty. Muslim tenets limited a man to four wives, but he could easily divorce one to make room for another. The way of life, needless to say, contrasted strongly with Western ways. The slower pace is influenced by the climate, which is hot and humid for most of the year. But we found it delightfully mild for two or three months in the wintertime. There was one rain in a year and a half, about two inches.

Our house, one of the few modern-type buildings in Jidda, was a small prefabricated air-conditioned structure in the city's outskirts. It was made in the Netherlands. It was furnished with fine oriental rugs and ornate furniture, comfortable but a bit incongruous for so modest a building. The house was one of a group in the Bechtel "compound." The Bechtel Company of San Francisco had built part of the pipeline from the oil area to the Mediterranean and currently was engaged in doing engineering work for the government. The company ran a well-stocked commissary from which we could buy groceries and other supplies shipped from New York. Also, the company had an excellent mess, from which we could order for our house meals or the main course as desired. That made entertaining easy. We engaged a Saudi houseboy, Hersey, who knew some English.

Social life in Jidda was simple and pleasant, with the small foreign community and many local people. Formal dress for men was the "Red Sea kit." This consisted of the lower half of ordinary formal attire with cummerbund and a short-sleeved white shirt open-necked and with no tie—a style that could be recommended for summer use at home. We brought from New York a tropicalized piano that I played. It was the only usable piano in Jidda, and it helped to make our home something of a center for informal gatherings. Luckily, I had brought along tuning equipment, which had to be used almost weekly to keep the piano usable in the trying damp climate, despite having an electric light constantly going inside the piano to promote dryness. We extended hospitality to many members of the foreign and local communities who enjoyed music and singing together.

Pleasant diversions were collecting seashells, of which there was a great variety, and swimming in the warm water of the Red Sea, buoyant with heavy salt concentration. We foreigners swam at an isolated spot. But some men from Jidda would gather at a discreet distance to look at the foreign women entering and leaving the water in their scanty bathing suits. Friday picnics often took place on a quarantine island in the Red Sea, where Italian internees and other prisoners were held after defeat in Ethiopia during World War II. The swimming was excellent.

At Christmas we were able to gather from the desert enough greenery for a synthetic Christmas tree. It fell to my lot to arrange quartets and other music for informal celebrations of Christmas and Easter at the American Embassy. Public non-Muslim services were not allowed.

Alcoholic drinks were taboo. At the time of our arrival they were allowed for foreigners. But on September 22, 1952 (Muharram 2, 1372, per the Muslim calendar), the king issued the following decree (American Embassy translation):

We, Abdul Aziz Ibn Abdul Rahman Al-Faysal, King of Saudi Arabia, Relying on God, and since Our country is an Islamic country following the Mohammedan Law, and in view of the fact that Our law has prohibited alcoholic beverages and considers it the cause of all atrocities and the foundation for every vice; and since it has reached our knowledge that the use of alcoholic beverages has spread in the country through its importation by persons who have been tolerated because they are Non-Moslems, which fact has led to a great corruption;

Therefore, in execution of Islamic Law, We have peremptorily ordered the forbidding of importation of all kinds of alcoholic beverages into the Kingdom by anyone whomsoever, whether Moslem or Non-Moslem, native or foreigner. He who disobeys Our order shall be subject to severe punishment; a native convicted of bringing in alcoholic beverages shall be lashed one hundred times and sentenced for one year in jail—a Non-Saudi shall be expelled as soon as he is convicted.

This decree followed the case of a prince who shot a British vice-consul in an affair rumored to have involved liquor. The king offered to execute the prince if Britain so desired—a request that naturally was not made. That prince had been at a party (without liquor) at our house not long before, at which he played the guitar and had a good time.

It was most fortunate that Ray Hare was the American ambassador during my stay. He was an ideal ambassador. His solid judgment, integrity, and affability were buttressed by long experience in the Middle East and knowledge of Arabic. I relied greatly on his wise advice as to how best to proceed in a delicate situation. He advised a cautious and gradual approach, which fitted in with my own predilection as to how best to work in similar situations. He had at heart the best interests of Saudi Arabia as well as of America.

Two hours after my arrival the ambassador took me to call on Finance Minister Shaykh Abd Allah Sulayman, then in his sixties. He was impressive and dignified in his white robe. He did not speak English. The embassy's bright young interpreter was Muhammad Ibrahim Mas'ud, who later became minister of state in the Council

Finance Minister Shaykh Abd Allah Sulayman (taken by the author)

of Ministers. Shaykh Abd Allah warmly welcomed me, saying that he looked forward to my help with financial problems. I promised to be at his disposal in all such matters.

One or two days later, Ambassador Hare took me to call officially on then Foreign Minister Prince Faysal. He impressed me greatly with his strong personality and obvious ability. He hoped that my coming would lead to worthwhile reforms. He remarked that he was pro-American but did not like the American policy of favoring Israel over the Arabs. He thus emphasized a deeply felt and consistent Saudi Arabian attitude.

King Faysal ibn Abd al-Aziz, 1905–1975 (courtesy of Aramco World Magazine)

ABD AL-AZIZ AND HIS GOVERNMENT

I soon had the honor of being presented to His Majesty King Abd al-Aziz. Assistant Deputy Minister of Finance Najib Bey Salihah called to tell me that the next day a special plane of the Saudi Arabian Air Lines, now known as Saudia, which was then run by TWA, would take us to Taif where I would be presented to the king at his summer palace. It was a privilege to go to Taif because few non-Muslims went there at that time. Taif is about one hundred miles southeast of Jidda and a mile above sea level on the eastern side of mountains that rise in the vicinity to over 8,000 feet. The direct route was over Mecca. But we made a detour to avoid overflying the sacred city.

We landed on an airstrip on naturally hard desert ground. Driving over a hill, we looked down into a valley with hundreds of tents, laid out in streets near the palace. It was an oasis with date palms and some large shrubs but with few trees. In some respects, the sight was similar to what might have been seen in the days of Abraham, except for electric wiring and an occasional truck contrasting with the camel trains, donkeys, and goats. The king traveled to Taif in his private DC-3, a gift from President Roosevelt, from his capital at Riyadh near the geographical center of the Arabian peninsula. A horde of about 2,000 guards and retainers followed the king—a few by air but most by motor car or camel caravan across the desert. In their tents they lived off his bounty.

I was conducted to Shaykh Abd Allah Sulayman's tent. It was about 25 feet square, with a double canvas roof and openings on three sides in the center of each side. It was pleasantly cool. The floor was covered with handsome oriental rugs. The finance minister sat in the middle, with a chair on his right and a small table with telephone between the two chairs. He received me cordially, and we had a conference lasting till noon—I having arrived about the middle of the morning.

After seeing the minister I was shown to my tent, of similar size and construction. It contained a table, a chair, and a bed. In an adjoining tent was a desk, which I could use as an office. Before long, Najib Bey Salihah came to take me to lunch, served in a tent nearby. There were about eight courses, some of which were superb.

About 4:00 P.M. a car came to take us to the palace. I wore a white suit, but for later audiences I used Arab dress—sets of which were presented by the king, the heir apparent, Prince Saud, and Shaykh Abd Allah Sulayman. The palace was a large roomy building with plenty of ventilation. I was met by the king's chamberlain and escorted to the minister of finance, who was waiting on the porch. After a few minutes word came that the king would see us.

The audience room was a high-ceilinged hall just to the right as one entered the palace. His Majesty's seat, ornamented with gold and covered with leopard skins, was at the far end of the room. The walls were lined with heavy couches with rich red coverings, and large, handsome oriental rugs covered the floor. Open windows on two sides gave a cooling breeze. Princes and courtiers were seated on the couches. Soldiers of the palace guard were kneeling around the entrance and inside the room.

The minister escorted me down the center of the hall, kneeled, kissed the king's hand, and presented me. Abd al-Aziz offered me his hand, which I shook, and I then made a low bow. The king motioned me to the seat at his right. The minister remained kneeling, as did Najib who interpreted.

Abd al-Aziz was then seventy years old, an impressive figure, about six feet four inches tall and with a powerful frame. In long years of desert fighting he had suffered many wounds and was lame and in poor health. He had lost an eye, reportedly from an infection. But his good eye was keen and penetrating. His mustache and beard were still mostly black. He wore a white robe and a red and white head-shawl with gold headropes. Altogether, he was of great dignity and imposing presence.

The interview was cordial but formal. No business was talked, as was the practice at first interviews. The king's first remark was, "It is cool here, isn't it." I agreed and told him that I found the climate of Taif delightful—and that in fact Jidda's climate so far was not too bad despite its reputation. He inquired about my trip from the United States, the route I had taken, and when I had arrived. He also asked where my home was and beamed when I mentioned California, then the most distant state. There were various pauses in the conversation, as the king was very deliberate. He spoke of his appreciation of the American government's sending me to Arabia. I assured him that it was a high privilege to work with His Majesty's government and that I would help in any way I could.

Meanwhile, the ceremony of serving coffee was under way. A

brightly dressed attendant came with a brass coffee pot with a long thin spout. Taking a small cup in his left hand, he raised the pot high above the cup and poured out the exact amount needed to fill the cup without spilling a drop. I dislike coffee but of course swallowed the cardamom-flavored mixture—I would have eaten a sheep's eye if offered, a choice morsel according to the hospitality of the desert tribesmen. Had any coffee been left in the cup, it would have been thrown on the rug.

After a time His Majesty indicated that the audience was ended. I rose and bowed and he offered me his hand. I then backed away from the royal presence, to the side, and left the room—bowing again at the door. In this I followed the example of the minister. The minister conducted me to the plane. We reached Jidda just at sunset. It had been quite a day.

King Abd al-Aziz was a great leader. Welding Arabia's warring tribes into a peaceful and orderly nation must rank as one of the most remarkable nation-building feats of modern times. Numerous writers have told of his life and work. Derek Hopwood listed many such books,[3] and the list is not complete. The king's most assiduous "Boswell" was Philby, whose relation to him was unique. In *Arabian Jubilee*, Philby gives full details of his rise to power and his varied activities and accomplishments, including dealings with his fellow Arabs and foreigners and his prowess with women, which was always strictly in keeping with the precepts of the Koran.

He ruled as a patriarchic monarch, keeping everything important in his own hands. Elizabeth Monroe tells of the visit of a British mission in 1917, during World War I, when Abd al-Aziz was thirty-seven years old:

The mission found Ibn Saud an indefatigable worker, giving audiences, hearing petitions, judging cases, arguing with his visitors, pausing only for prayer, from dawn until far into the night. . . . He seemed able to do with very little sleep. . . . They found him a voluble talker, unfamiliar with Western ways of thought, but a hard bargainer, and of course, well versed in desert politics.[4]

Sir Reader Bullard, who as British minister knew him in his prime in the years between the wars, said his "most remarkable quality was his political wisdom,'' which grew after ''dealing with self-willed, hasty Arab tribesmen . . . until it was equal to any situation.'' By following closely Arabic broadcasts from Europe and Cairo, Abd al-Aziz ''managed to be better informed on international affairs than many educated Europeans.''[5] His feat of unifying his country, together with his powerful personality, caused him to stand head and shoulders above his fellow countrymen. He was recognized as an outstanding leader in the Arab world.

Abd al-Aziz, like his successors today, continued making himself accessible to his subjects to dispense justice at his daily *majlis*, or audience, at which even a humble desert tribesman could bring a complaint. But growing volume and his weakening health eventually led him to restrict this practice. The law was based on the Koran. Since punishment for serious theft could lead to the cutting off of a hand, property was notably safe.

Years of arduous living and battle had taken their toll on the king. In the spring of 1950, he was in a wheelchair and an American medical mission came to treat him. They relieved the swelling and stiffness of his legs, so that he could move around with considerable ease. Fred H. Awalt of the State Department, who was with the mission, reported that the king had noticeably failed in the five years since he had seen him.[6]

Finance Minister Shaykh Abd Allah Sulayman was a native of Unayzah, in the northern part of Nejd. Unayzah was the junction of two main trade routes and hence was more cosmopolitan than most inland places. A small man, he had to be tough and durable to have managed Abd al-Aziz's finances and helped with supply and transport during the years of desert fighting, and somehow to have made ends meet during the difficult years before oil became important.

In his youth he had lived in India for several years. He is said to have worked for a time in a coffee shop in Bombay and to have taken a course in accountancy. He returned to Arabia, where his elder brother was Abd al-Aziz's secretary. When the brother died in the mid-1920s, he took over the job.

Readiness to take responsibility broadened his work. He soon won the king's trust and became his paymaster. Also he took an active part in supply of the armies during Abd al-Aziz's campaign that overthrew the Hashimite King Husayn and gained the Jidda-Mecca region. He supervised the introduction of new coins there.

He had Abd al-Aziz's full confidence in matters of finance and administration. Abd Allah Sulayman's executive ability and energy led him to become the country's most powerful man outside the royal family. After unification he gradually spread the use of Saudi currency throughout the country. He established revenue offices in the provinces and set the rates of internal taxes and customs duties. He played a crucial role in finding the money that helped prosecute the brief and successful Yemen war of 1934. His part in this operation secured him even more firmly in the king's confidence.

Since he paid the bills, he gained power over other departments. He became responsible for public projects such as improvement of water resources and construction of ports and airports. He promoted the successful agricultural development at al-Kharj, near Riyadh. As indicating his authority it is told that after the war, while talking in Jidda with an engineer of Bechtel Company, which was to build the port improvements, the question arose of where to get the fill. He ordered the old city walls torn down. Dynamite was placed, and the walls fell down like those of Jericho.[7]

He was shrewd and tough in handling negotiations with foreign interests, notably the oil concession of 1933 and the hard bargaining in 1950 that led to increasing Aramco's payments to a 50/50 basis. Abd al-Aziz sent him to the United States after the war to try to get a loan for the proposed railway from the oil area to Riyadh, a project the king had long desired. As transactions in foreign currency grew, he set up a state account in New York in his own name, and he also had a personal account there. But as oil revenue grew, exchange transactions were handled mainly through the branch of the Netherlands Trading Society at Jidda.

Shaykh Abd Allah was absolutely devoted to Abd al-Aziz and humble in his presence. He realized that in matters of spending the heavy demands of the king and princes had priority, without accounting. Thus, he financed the royal household and the activities the king handled such as security, defense, religious affairs, and upkeep of his retainers. Shaykh Abd Allah administered what was left, largely according to his discretion.

He was conscious of the need for restraint, especially when oil revenue grew. I have already told of his experience with the 1947 budget, when the king rejected proposed economies (Chapter 3). But he persisted, and when we arrived, there was a budget for the fiscal year ending March 25, 1952, including items for the royal family. At times he was independent enough to act on his own, hoping that it would work out. He lived well and prospered, maintaining ample establishments at Riyadh, Jidda, and Mecca.

I was fortunate to establish good relations with Shaykh Abd Allah and win his confidence early in my stay. I always found him considerate. He knew that his technical understanding of currency and fiscal problems was limited and was ready to accept help. He was quick to grasp my proposals for a national bank and my analysis of the country's currency problems. It was gratifying that he readily agreed with my proposed solutions and was ready to make decisions. The ability of an authoritative regime to act made possible giving effect to change without undue delay.

THE WORK PROCEEDS

A room in our house served as my office, since no other suitable place was then available. The usual work hours were from 7:00 A.M. to 2:00 P.M. The government arranged for me to have as assistant and interpreter Fu'ad Najjar, an intelligent and personable Lebanese who spoke excellent English. (Later I met him and his attractive family in Lebanon; I hope that the troubles in 1982 in that unhappy country have left them unscathed.) A new Chrysler car and a driver were also provided. Najib Bey Salihah asked me for a list of office supplies needed. After I provided the list the lesser official charged with the matter tried to make petty reductions. As the list was modest and the items available, I felt I had to insist on no changes to avoid future trouble. The items were duly provided. Because my prospective stay was not long, I did not try to learn Arabic, a difficult language, other than the numerals. But Mrs. Young exchanged Arabic lessons for English with Najib's attractive Lebanese wife, since the Salihahs lived nearby. She did not speak English, and French was their language in common.

My first task, as in other such assignments, was to try as promptly as possible to understand the situation, and to gain the leaders' confidence. The government at last could provide a budget, for the current period, with English translation. The total was equivalent to about $135 million, for the fiscal year 1370–71 (April 8, 1951–March 25, 1952). It showed an increase of 130 percent over the abortive budget of three years earlier, for which comparable figures were shown. But the government could provide little information about the economy other than some data of foreign trade. To get a line on prices, I had Fu'ad Najjar go to the *suq* twice weekly to gather data to begin a simple price index.

I moved quickly to get acquainted with the local community, Saudi and foreign. I met leading businessmen and Finance Ministry officials. British Ambassador Clinton Pelham, whom I had known years before in China, was friendly and helpful. Also, I met members of the British Locust Control Mission. Later, when temporarily acting as director of the American aid mission, I found myself reporting on the locust situation in and near Saudi Arabia. The managers of the foreign banks were cooperative and helpful, especially Messrs. D. Entrop Philipp and Husayn al-Attas of the Dutch bank and M. De Precourt of the French. Records of those two long-established banks supplemented data from Aramco about exchange rates. Frequently I called on the managers to discuss developments.

Aramco, with its large-scale operations, had a special interest in improvement of the financial system. The company's officers were helpful to me throughout my stay. Garry Owen, in charge of the Jidda office, was in effect a diplomatic representative of the company in dealing with SAG. He, his assistant Robert N. Henry, and R. S. Hawkey, the Aramco financial specialist, were always cooperative— Hawkey being the only specialist in the country with whom I could discuss technical monetary problems. Less often I had helpful contact with W. F. Moore, president of Aramco, and with F. W. Ohliger, vice-president.

As soon as practicable after arrival in Jidda, I accepted Aramco's invitation to visit the oil area, 750 miles to the northeast. The headquarters is at Dhahran, close to the eastern shore. Traveling in an Aramco DC-3, we saw in the desert an impressive complex of oil wells, storage tanks, machinery, shops, and a refinery. Surplus gas was flared from pipes high in the air—a waste now largely corrected. An American-type village at Dhahran housed the many hundreds of American employees. Aramco was making a good record in training Saudi Arabians for all kinds of work: mechanical, clerical, and technical. It was gratifying to see Saudi Arabians operating many kinds of light and heavy mechanical equipment and doing technical accounting and secretarial work. There were about 14,000 Saudi Arabian employees in 1951, plus many from other Arab states. Aramco had a broad community program. It encouraged Saudi employees to own their homes by financing the costs on favorable terms. For the Arab community it provided sanitary facilities, running water, electricity, hospitals and clinics, recreational facilities, schools, and mosques. It helped local businessmen to become contractors or to produce many kinds of goods needed in the oil operation and in the country generally. All in all, Aramco's policy was enlightened and beneficial to Saudi Arabia.

After we were shown the oil installations and told about the operations and the financial problems, we were flown to neighboring Bahrain Island. The Shaykhdom of Bahrain was a well-run mini-state where, at the time, Britain attended to foreign affairs and finance, leaving domestic affairs to the local authorities. After inspecting the oil operations there (where oil was discovered in 1932), I had a useful talk with the British adviser.

Especially interesting was a trip across the desert to the remarkable oasis of al-Hufuf, the largest in the country. There we saw water gushing from perennial artesian springs, fed underground from distant mountains to the west. We were told that the flow was more than 15,000 gallons per minute. We saw water being raised, by donkey power, to be distributed at higher levels. The donkeys, urged on by a boy, walked down an incline, turned, and climbed back pulling small buckets of water, which were then dumped into an irrigation ditch. Much water was also raised by manpower, using the age-old method of raising buckets on long poles with counterweights. There were thousands of date palms and fruit trees and fields of growing grain and vegetables.

The central castle of al-Hufuf was a striking sight with its huge mud walls and massive round turrets. There we had lunch with the governor, Amir Saud ibn Abd Allah ibn Jalwi (coloquially, Jiluwi), the son of the cousin who had saved Abd al-Aziz's life at the taking of Riyadh fifty years earlier. When we saw al-Hufuf from the air upon returning from Dhahran to Jidda, the contrast between the lush growth and the surrounding desert was striking.

There were even freshwater springs in the Gulf some distance east of al-Hufuf. Traditionally, divers with camel-skin bags dived down in relays until the skins were filled and closed. Aramco tapped an undersea spring for fresh water when the search for oil began under the 1933 concession.

From the beginning of my stay in Saudi Arabia it was clear that a solid reform of the country's finances was going to depend upon devising the right kind of bank to manage the government's receipts and payments and operate a stable and convenient monetary system. Careful investigation and analysis were going to be needed before making practicable proposals. This was going to take time. Thus, I tried to act according to the Arab proverb: "Be as a doctor who does not hurry with a remedy before knowing the disease."

On one matter, however, I could move quickly. The government was living well beyond its means, despite the great flow of oil revenue and income tax. Payments of income tax were made only quarterly, and the government pressed Aramco for advances. Also, it borrowed heavily from banks to anticipate revenue and was slow to pay its contractors and suppliers. I worked out a procedure for monthly payments with Aramco and the government without difficulty. This change brought some improvement but did not of course cure extravagance and waste.

Since the government was beginning to receive shipments of the new Saudi gold sovereigns from France, it was anxious to know what to do with them. In a preliminary report to the finance minister I explained that there was no dependable way to tie together full-weight gold and silver coins. There were wide variations of the ratio between gold and silver in world markets. Thus, in previous years this had varied between about 100–1 and 45–1. As to linking the riyal to the dollar, silver prices had recently ranged between 45 and 90 cents per ounce. Gold in free markets had ranged between about $38 and $100 per ounce. Foreign gold coins had varied widely, with premiums well above the gold parity of $35 per ounce. But fiduciary coins could be given stable values if limited to the public's need for them and guaranteed free convertibility. In October I told Shaykh Abd Allah that the International Monetary Fund had decided to allow gold-producing countries to sell gold freely above the $35 price and that I was studying the bearing of this upon issuance of the new gold coin. The upshot was telling him that serious monetary reform should await founding the proposed bank. The bank was not to begin operations until the fall of 1952.

While I was giving priority to investigating and analyzing the problems of creating the bank and reforming the currency, the work of the experts on tariff, customs procedure, budget, and accounting went forward. As mentioned in an earlier chapter, before the days of oil the tariff, along with pilgrim dues, had been a major source of revenue. Saudi Arabia needed to import many items of food, clothing, machinery, and building materials for the people's welfare and progress. Hence a properly adjusted tariff and a smooth-working customs administration were important. The king and his advisers had felt for some time that the tariff should be made less burdensome and its operation improved. This led to the request that the financial mission include experts on these matters.

Staff experts Kennedy and Dunaway were well received and given full opportunity to work. Their work bore valuable fruit in adoption of a new tariff, which took effect about December 1, 1952. This provided for free entry for some important items such as drugs and medicines, books and periodicals, agricultural implements and fertilizer. Some of these were freed from duty earlier during 1951–52. Low rates were placed on items needed by the masses such as cereals and cheap cloth. Duties were reduced on items needed for development. Surtaxes, of which there were about ten, were consolidated into a single surtax. For greater fairness some items were transferred from specific rates on units to an ad valorem basis. Rates on luxury imports were raised. Exemption from duties for various officials was ended; the privilege had been abused. Export duties were abolished.

Customs procedures had been enormously complicated and obstructive. There was a system of "visitors' books." An importer had to take a book of forms and get more than twenty signatures of various officials to learn the amount of duty and clear the goods. Infinite possibilities of delay made for corruption. Since a book was used for a number of transactions, an individual importer was denied privacy as to quantities and costs. Dunaway devised a bill of entry containing the particulars needed by the customs administration and the importer. He also proposed changes in organization and procedures. His recommendations, along with the new tariff, led to improvements that simplified and promoted foreign trade and led to lower living costs for the people.

Growing income from oil also made possible some relief for pilgrims from abroad. They had been charged a fee of £28 (about $78 in 1952) per head, collected at Saudi offices abroad. In May 1952 Abd al-Aziz ended this fee on his own initiative.

Because of the delay in sending an American accounting expert, the accountant, John Bode, did not arrive until after I had left Saudi Arabia in the fall of 1952. Meanwhile, the government engaged Fu'ad abu-Izz al-Din, a competent Lebanese accountant. He worked closely with our group and helped to devise the improved system for the customs.

When we arrived, the budget in effect was for the fiscal year ending March 25, 1952. The budget expert, John A. Stacy, did not arrive until well into that period, when the next budget was being prepared. He established good working arrangements with the budget officers of the Finance Ministry, a number of whom were devoted to budgetary progress. He helped them to improve both the form and the substance of the new budget. He also helped with procedures of control. But moves for more effective control had to await setting up the Saudi Arabian Monetary Agency in October 1952, to become the government's fiscal agent.

The new budget called for outlay equivalent to about $205 million—a far cry from the $7 million of fifteen years earlier. (A summary is shown in Appendix I, Table 6.) Regardless of budgets, the government was still living well beyond its means. Despite rapid growth of oil revenue, it continued to discount future receipts.

There was an ambitious program of development, in which there was great and growing interest. One project, later dropped, was for a railway from Jidda to Riyadh. The program called for new roads from Mecca to Taif, from Jidda to Medina, and in areas around Jidda and Riyadh. Port improvements at Jidda and Dammam were to continue. Projects included improving water resources at Jidda, Mecca, Medina, and Riyadh and constructing sewer systems in leading cities. Plans included building hospitals and mosques. Also, airports were to be developed. Estimated costs totaled about $350 million.[8]

There was little that either a mission of foreigners or like-minded officials of the Finance Ministry could do about the excessive spending already mentioned. I did not feel it wise to discuss economy with King Abd al-Aziz or the heir apparent, Saud, unless a good opening came up, which never happened. I would have risked impairing my usefulness in other fields. I used every suitable occasion, however, to urge on Shaykh Abd Allah and lesser officials the importance of economy and of using the greater part of the oil monies for economic and social improvement. Also, I stressed the need to set up large financial reserves.

THE AMERICAN AID PROGRAM

Toward the end of 1951 I got word that I would be put on the American government's roll instead of being paid by Saudi Arabia. I would become a part of the Technical Cooperation Administration (TCA), the office for foreign aid under President Truman's Point Four program. I was to be appointed a Foreign Service Reserve Officer, Class I. The State Department tried to arrange the rank of minister, because the added prestige would help in my work. I had chosen to go to Saudi Arabia rather than accept a post as aid director in a larger country with that rank. But TCA would not agree to that rank for a different post in a small country. In Washington, TCA had authorized the State Department to tell me that I would have a 25 percent "unhealthy post" allowance on salary. But, for reasons best known to the bureaucracy, that did not materialize, and after argument I accepted the appointment.

Washington offered to Saudi Arabia an aid program, and a basic agreement was concluded in 1951. Emissaries from TCA then came to Saudi Arabia to discuss the program. This was to include help in agriculture, water resources, health, and education. With the emissaries I went to Riyadh for the discussions, which resulted in agreement concerning the program. The emissaries asked me to head the program in addition to the financial mission. I declined because I did not plan to stay in the country, but I finally agreed to act temporarily until a permanent head could come.

I soon found that Washington had made elaborate plans, calling for a program officer, an assistant program officer, an executive officer, a property and supply officer, an administrative assistant for the director, a secretary-stenographer (in addition to the lady who was helping me), two clerk-stenographers, and one file clerk.

Housing available in Jidda was barely enough for the three American experts already working on the country's water problems. Electricity, air conditioning, and water were scarce. Caring for more experts would be difficult, and bringing a group of added people for administration would be absurd. For the foreseeable future the director would need no more than a secretary-stenographer and an administrative assistant. Thus, I rejected the proposed structure and got away with it. While this was going on Washington offered to send me someone as a legal adviser! I quickly turned that down; I was a lawyer, as was Kennedy, and none of us could help much in matters of Islamic law. Later, while visiting other Middle East countries, I found that administrators were about as numerous as experts in the aid missions.

Also, toward the end of the fiscal year on June 30, I was told that an unexpended balance of funds was available—could I spend it? I replied that there was no need to do so. I pointed out that our group was trying to induce Saudi Arabia to organize its affairs efficiently and economically and to curb waste. These efforts would be impaired if our own government did not do likewise. I expressed the hope that similar care would be used in staffing aid missions elsewhere, pointing out that Herbert Hoover's overstaffing of Commerce Department offices abroad had led to overly deep cuts when the Roosevelt administration took over in 1933. Because I was not making a career in the aid program, I could more readily object as "an American taxpayer." Nevertheless, when I returned to Washington the director of the Point Four program asked me to take another job as a country director, which I declined.

In due course the newly appointed aid director arrived, and I was glad to turn over responsibility to him. But soon I was shocked to learn from the aid people in Washington that, at the very time when the Monetary Agency was being readied for opening, I was named "Chief, Public Administration and Government Service, Field Party" under the new director instead of continuing separately as head of the financial mission. Before leaving Washington I had been promised that in Saudi Arabia I would be the ranking American officer in financial and economic matters. I was dealing with the king, the heir apparent, and the finance minister. In previous similar assignments in Latin America and China, I had dealt with heads of state and cabinet officers. To become even technically subordinate to an intermediary was a demotion I refused to accept. Fortunately, I could drag along the situation without embarrassment to the United States and without impairing my position vis-à-vis Saudi Arabia until the Monetary Agency successfully opened and I could leave. But I was not happy with the episode in view of what the financial mission was accomplishing.

After I left, the financial work continued on the new basis under Dunaway's direction. For personal reasons the country director did not last long, and Dunaway became acting director. The aid program was expanded somewhat in agriculture, public health, and education. It continued until Saudi Arabia decided to engage directly such experts as were desired.

5

FOUNDING THE SAUDI ARABIAN MONETARY AGENCY

From time to time before 1951 Abd al-Aziz and his councilors had the idea that Saudi Arabia ought to have a national bank. Some of my predecessors had also seen the need for this but felt that the time was not ripe. Thus, years of talk had led to no concrete result. Now the time for action had come. When the king asked for American help in 1950, he stressed the need for a government bank, not only to stabilize the currency internally and in foreign exchange, but also to handle the government's exchange transactions and money transfers. Finance Minister Abd Allah Sulayman reinforced this view at our first meeting, when he asked me to study the possible creation of a national bank.

The minister again spoke of the bank two weeks later in Taif, when I was summoned there to be presented to the king. I explained that the problems were so important and complex that I wanted to study the situation thoroughly before making recommendations. In other countries, I pointed out, such studies extended over considerable time. But I would report to him as soon as I could, after assuring myself that the plan proposed would be in the country's best interests.

Various ideas had been proposed about what a new bank should be and do. An abortive idea of the 1930s contemplated a Saudi-foreign bank that would profitably handle expected oil revenue. The British project of a Currency Board, to issue notes backed by 100 percent reserve, had been dropped. In 1951 several schemes were being more or less seriously considered. In May, Delaby of the Banque de l'Indochine proposed a "Stabilization Administration" under the Finance Ministry, to handle monetary reform. If it worked well it could be converted into a national bank with broader functions. The Netherlands Trading Society (NTS) had a strategic position because it did most of the foreign exchange business for the government. This resulted from the fact that NTS handled the financial affairs of the large flow of pilgrims from Java. It was considering a scheme for having a 55 percent interest in a national bank, which it would manage for five years pending a shift to Saudi interests. NTS and the local firm known as Ka'ki Salih (Abd al-Aziz Al al-Ka'ki and Salim ibn Mahfuz Company) handled most money transfers within the country. There were suggestions that local financial and commercial interests participate in setting up such a bank. In government circles some officials, seeing the profitability of local banks, thought of a bank as a source of profit and as a source of credit that would help solve the government's financial problems. Clearly, such ideas were bad. While talking with proponents of these schemes I was noncommittal, as I felt that none would be in Saudi Arabia's interest.

After several weeks of study I sent to Washington for comment a full analysis of the situation and a detailed plan for a government bank. I had no specific instructions from Washington about my work, but the record showed that in the past the experts of the State and Treasury departments were interested in reviewing such plans. Also, I wanted to know whether Washington would help to find an American to act as governor. On the latter I wrote:

SAG should engage a well-qualified foreigner to act as governor. SAG should contemplate having a foreign governor until such time as there is available a qualified Saudi Arabian national to take the post under conditions in which he could achieve the essential objects of the bank.

I stated that I did not want to become the governor. Although I had considerable experience in this field, I planned to return to the United States, and the governor perhaps should also succeed me as financial adviser. I thought it better to look for someone who had actually managed a central bank. My leading candidate was George Blowers, whom I knew. He had headed central banks in Liberia and Ethiopia and was then with the International Monetary Fund. He was in fact later to become the first governor.

My analysis pointed out that the existing financial machinery was inadequate. Oil revenue had grown so fast in the preceding three years that "there has not been time to develop proper machinery to handle receipts and payments." What sufficed for a country with a budget of about $7 million could not handle a budget more than twenty times as great. Foreign exchange had become a major problem, since about five sixths of the revenue was in foreign currency.

There was no adequate machinery to handle monetary affairs, such as to introduce the new gold coin or provide a convenient system of other coins "limited to needs of the circulation and convertible into a standard unit." There was no way to regulate local banking or moneychanging. There was no machinery for economic research, which was necessary "to help the government in formulating and carrying out wise financial and economic policy." I included a preliminary suggestion about handling economic development.

Government banks in other countries commonly created credit "by issue of circulating notes and by loans to the government." As to this I said that "the abuses of this function in even the strongest and most experienced countries have been and are so great that it would be dangerous, in my opinion, for Saudi Arabia to undertake this now or in the near future."

While awaiting comment from Washington, Shaykh Abd Allah pressed me for the report. Having no reply after six weeks, and being confident of my conclusions, I decided to proceed on my own responsibility. So I sent him on November 14 a detailed plan as a preliminary report, in English with Arabic translation. Another six weeks later I had word that the experts in Washington agreed in general with the plan, which had been caught in the toils of interdepartmental procedure. They specifically endorsed my views about banning circulating notes and loans and stressed that the setup should safeguard the institution's independence vis-à-vis the government. They agreed that Blowers would be an excellent choice as governor.

My preliminary report to Shaykh Abd Allah said:

Most countries today have such institutions of one kind or another. They provide machinery that is necessary for the operation of a stable and convenient monetary system. They afford means to regulate local monetary and banking practices as may be appropriate. They make easier the handling of public receipts and payments and holding and transfer of funds. They give close and regular contact with financial centers. They collect and analyze data about local and foreign financial conditions and are thus in position to advise the Government on important problems.

To exercise these functions I proposed creating the "Saudi Arabian National Bank," for which the government would provide the capital.

The final plan for the Saudi Arabian Monetary Agency was substantially the same as that given to Shaykh Abd Allah. Some changes and additions resulted from my discussions with the king, the heir apparent, Shaykh Abd Allah, and other high personages. The report and the royal decree of April 1952 sanctioning the charter of the Agency are reprinted in Appendixes II and III, respectively.

Shaykh Abd Allah told me two weeks after receiving my report that he approved the plan and had sent it to the king at Riyadh. In January he said that the king and his advisers agreed in principle with the plan. But that was only the start of the effort to put the plan into operation. In mid-February, George Blowers arrived in Jidda. He was in Athens on business for the International Monetary Fund, and I had arranged for his visit. Shaykh Abd Allah asked us both to come to Riyadh.

Riyadh in 1949, the marketplace (courtesy of Aramco)

DECISION AT RIYADH

Riyadh in 1952 differed vastly from the burgeoning city it has become today. Its aspect then was still that of capital of a desert country, with camels much in evidence. Abd al-Aziz's palace was an impressive structure with thick crenellated mud walls. On a previous visit, to discuss the American aid program, I had been honored by being a guest in the palace. It was an honor to visit, but if truth be told it was less comfortable than the Bechtel compound where Blowers and I later stayed.

The city and its surroundings were beginning the immense alterations then just getting under way as part of the great and growing affluence. The heir apparent, Amir Saud ibn Abd al-Aziz had an elaborate palace, newer than that of the king, outside the city. He

Old palace in Riyadh, 1952; the author and interpreter (taken by Thomas A. Hart)

was the king's eldest living son and came to the throne when his father died in 1953. An older brother, Amir Turki, had died in the influenza epidemic of 1919. Amir Saud's extensive gardens were ornamented by a variety of plants and trees. King Abd al-Aziz had more than forty sons, and some of their lesser palaces lined a street near the palace.

Amir Saud was, like his father, a kindly man, and I enjoyed his hospitality on several occasions. He invited Blowers and me to a dinner on this occasion for the shaykh of Qatar, who was making a state visit. About forty of us entered the palace room and washed our hands at the rows of washstands along the walls. We seated ourselves on the floor on a huge oriental rug, surrounding a tablecloth that groaned with food. There were three roast young camels, fifteen roast sheep, a roast chicken at each place, platters of saffron rice and other vegetables, dishes of canned fruits, and glasses of camel's milk. The servants girded up their loins, tucking the surplus white cloth into their belts; drew their swords; stepped past the guests; and carved the camels, sheep, and chickens. We ate with the right hand only—the left being reserved for unclean activities—but knives, forks, and spoons were also provided.

When Blowers and I arrived at Riyadh, along with Najib Bey Salihah, who interpreted, we were taken to Shaykh Abd Allah's house for lunch. He told us that the important people in Riyadh, from the king down, wished the institution to be set up along the lines of my plan. But in some quarters there was concern about the possibility that the institution would charge or receive interest, contrary to the Islamic law. Shaykh Abd Allah said that the king and the heir apparent were likely to question me about interest and the Islamic law. If they did not bring up the subject, he wished me to do so and to reassure them.

I stated that I fully understood the Islamic view about interest on money lent or invested, that I had never contemplated that the institution should do anything in disregard of Islamic law, that the charter could specifically state that the institution would neither pay nor receive interest, and that I would be happy to make this quite clear to His Majesty and the heir apparent.

Shaykh Abd Allah further pointed out that the name of the institution had caused some concern, because the word "bank" was associated with interest. I stated that the institution could be called "Financial Agency," if preferred. Shaykh Abd Allah believed this would be desirable. (It was later decided to call it "Monetary Agency.")

The same afternoon Blowers and I had an audience with His Majesty. The audience was intended to be private, but before we arrived the shaykh of Qatar, who was the king's guest, came into the courtroom. With the shaykh present the king did not bring up any item of business but merely engaged in some general conversation with us. The interpreter, Abd Allah Tariqi (an American-educated petroleum geologist in the Ministry of Finance), told us that the king had said to the shaykh that he had asked the American government for the help of some financial experts and that "Americans are very good in matters of accounting and currency." The king closed the interview by saying that he wished to see us privately.

After the state dinner in honor of the shaykh of Qatar, the heir apparent told me that he wished to see us the next day for a discussion. After dinner the king's adviser, Jamal al-Husayni, had a short discussion with us. He said that he and the others there thought the general plan of the institution was good and that, if the point about interest were covered, there should be no objections of consequence.

The next day Blowers and I went over in detail the plan of the proposed institution as outlined in my report of November 14, 1951. We found ourselves in complete agreement. We also discussed at length my plan for currency reform and likewise found ourselves in agreement, subject to further consideration of some points.

The heir apparent invited us to luncheon. It was an elaborate meal and very good, as he had an American chef and imported refrigerated food from the United States. After luncheon we had a private discussion of the Agency with him. He stated that the plan had met with general acceptance in Riyadh but that there were four points that he would stress: (1) The head office should be in Riyadh. (2) The institution should receive all revenue, control all disbursements, and keep the government fully informed of its operations and position. The government should have monthly reports. The government would look to me to see to it that this was properly done. (3) The institution should not pay interest and must have full regard to the Islamic law. (4) The general plan of operation and the main personnel employed should be approved by Riyadh.

Amir Saud went on to say that everyone felt that the monetary situation ought to be improved. The losses and inconvenience resulting from monetary fluctuations were causing concern, and the government wanted a stable currency. It was anxious for better control of receipts and payments.

I stated that his comments showed that he clearly appreciated the needs of the country and the main work of the proposed institution, namely, to aid in better control of the public finances and to improve the currency situation. I expressed gratification that the government was disposed to take this important action. The organization, I stated, would of course keep such accounts as the government directed. As to the matter of interest, I told him basically what I had already said to Shaykh Abd Allah: that I well understood the Islamic law and that it had never been intended that the institution pay or receive interest. I added that a prohibition on this point could be included in the decree and the charter. Sensing that Shaykh Abd Allah would want the head office at Jidda, I only said to Amir Saud that of course the institution should keep the government fully informed of operations.

Later in the afternoon we were summoned to the palace to see the king. We were met by the finance minister, who stated that a further point had arisen with regard to the name. Some people felt that even the name "Financial Agency" suggested interest and transactions inconsistent with the spirit of Islamic law. I explained that the institution was to be a service agency that need not charge interest, since commission on government exchange transactions could easily cover operating costs. Also, another suitable name certainly could be found.

During the discussion, the question of the location of the head office arose. When talking with the heir apparent, I had refrained from commenting specifically on this point. The finance minister insisted, as I had anticipated, that the head office be at Jidda. I told him that obviously the main operations and preferably the head office should be there. I added that a similar question had arisen in other countries, where there was pressure to have the head office of the central bank in the capital. For example, in China the head office of the Central Bank had to be moved to Nanking, although the actual headquarters continued to be Shanghai. I said that I thought if necessary he could agree to put up a sign "Head Office" in Riyadh, that certain records could be kept there and meetings held there, but that the chief operations clearly should be at Jidda. The minister subsequently asked me for a letter on this subject. I wrote this in such a way as to avoid flatly taking sides between him and Amir Saud.

We did not see the king because the shaykh of Qatar again came in just when we were expected. They had a long talk and the king excused himself because he felt tired. A little later Shaykh Abd Allah went to the king's private quarters and had a talk he considered satisfactory, stating our views and covering the subjects we intended to discuss. We then returned to Jidda.

Two days later Shaykh Abd Allah sent word to me at eight o'clock in the morning that he wanted a draft decree and charter that afternoon, to be sent for the king's approval. With a secretary and translator at my elbow and in consultation with Blowers, I produced a brief enabling decree and a charter of twelve simple articles. These were duly delivered in midafternoon, in English and Arabic. This, I imagine, was some sort of record for speed in preparing a law to create a central bank. The task was easier because most points were in my report. Judd Polk of the American Treasury, who had investigated the situation in Saudi Arabia in 1948, wrote to me that he "was amazed at the brevity and simplicity of the Decree, compared to the sort of document that would be required for a similar thing in most countries."

The next day we went over the draft with the minister and Najib. They were generally satisfied, but the name "Financial Agency" still caused some difficulty. They suggested "Currency Institute." I explained that "Institute" would not do in English. We then agreed on "Monetary Agency." They proposed no other changes in the draft. They then referred the draft to the Egyptian legal adviser, Hani Khayr Allah, to check the Arabic wording.

Nevertheless, two more months and another visit to Riyadh were needed for final action. Part of the delay resulted from disagreement on the question of the location of the head office. The wording finally agreed upon was that "the main operating office in which it shall start its functions" was to be at Jidda, with branches and agencies "where required."

In April, King Abd al-Aziz summoned me to Riyadh, where Shaykh Abd Allah met me on arrival. He handed me two decrees dated 25 Rajab, 1371 (April 20, 1952), creating the Monetary Agency and sanctioning the charter. The text of the charter was my February draft with only minor changes (see Appendix III). But the king, said Shaykh Abd Allah, wanted further assurances before promulgating the decrees: that the Agency would be a constructive factor which would operate entirely in accordance with Islamic law.

At the audience with the king we found him in excellent spirits. When I asked about his health he said, "I am sure that I am stronger than you are." When I gave him the desired assurances he was pleased. For several minutes he spoke impressively about the Islamic law and its virtues, showing deep religious feeling. He also voiced appreciation of my work.

A week later the decrees of April 20, 1952, were published in the *Official Gazette*. Commenting on creation of the Agency, a writer in

The author with the decree of April 1952 chartering the Saudi Arabian Monetary Agency (taken by Mrs. Arthur N. Young)

a Mecca paper called it an example that "we take from what is new that which is good, and from the old that which is proper and correct." He praised the choice of the name "Agency"—in Arabic a word of deep resonance and captivating ringing instead of the gibberish word "bank."[1]

At Jidda in February I had recommended to Shaykh Abd Allah that he engage Blowers as the first governor of the Agency. To my embarrassment, he said: "I want you to do this." George said, "Go ahead if you wish." I expressed appreciation but said I strongly recommended Blowers. I said that, while I had had considerable central banking experience, I had never actually organized or run a bank, whereas Blowers had successfully headed such institutions in Liberia and Ethiopia. Also, I felt I should return to the United States. The minister then said that he considered it my general responsibility and would be disposed to accept anyone I recommended. This led to Blowers being appointed by royal decree.

FUNCTIONS OF THE AGENCY

In September 1952, the Finance Ministry published in Arabic and English, the important documents relating to creating the Agency. These included the royal decrees, the Agency's bylaws, and my report as revised to take account of the changes made at Riyadh.* Printing in English was a problem. The printer had only enough type for two pages and did not know English. So I had to read the proofs with unusual care; and he had to print two pages in English at a time before assembling the final copies.

The Agency's functions, and how it would exercise them for the benefit of the government and the economy, were analyzed in detail in the report. Operations would relate to currency affairs, fiscal agency functions, and financial and economic research.

---

*In this section, quotations (except as otherwise noted) and much of the coverage of the Agency's functions have been drawn directly from my report on the Monetary Agency, reprinted in its entirety in Appendix II. The commentary in this section is intended to provide the reader with a useful briefer statement of the main portions of the report, making clear the Agency's nature and important functions. Therefore, some technical particulars are not here included.

Currency Affairs. The charter provided that the Agency would have the following functions:

(a) To stabilize and maintain the external and internal value of the currency.

(b) To hold and operate any monetary reserve funds as separate funds earmarked for monetary purposes only.

(c) To buy and sell for Government account gold and silver coin and bullion.

(d) To advise the Government about new coinage and handle the manufacture, shipment and issue of all coins, it being understood that coins would be issued only through and at the request of the Agency.

(e) To regulate commercial banks, exchange dealers and money changers as may be found appropriate.

These clauses were designed to enable the Agency to regulate the foreign exchange value of the currency, to introduce the newly coined gold sovereign, and to clear the way for interconvertibility of the various coins and for other measures to improve the monetary and banking system.

Fiscal Agency Functions. The Finance Ministry appreciated the need for better budgetary control. Hence the importance of centralizing in the Agency the receipts of all branches of the government, and similarly of making all payments from accounts in the Agency. Thus, the Agency would hold all the government's operating funds in addition to monetary and fiscal reserves.

The Agency, it was pointed out, could be of great value as agent for the government to pay the budget and contractual obligations as per standing instructions. Of course, it would have to have sufficient funds. If a system of receipt of revenues and punctual payment, with priority of basic costs of government and of definitive contractual obligations, could be created through the Agency, the government's credit and the efficiency of its operations would notably improve. This procedure also would simplify administrative procedures and save much work for the Finance Ministry, and in particular for the minister and the highest officials of the ministry.

The report stressed the need to build up large fiscal reserves. It stated that the experience of Venezuela was significant as to handling large revenue from oil. Venezuela's total population was similar to that of Saudi Arabia, but its area was only about a third of that of Saudi Arabia, and its reserves of oil were large. Its production in 1940 was about 500,000 barrels daily, but in 1952 had risen to about 1.7 million daily (about twice what Saudi Arabia then produced). In 1940 Venezuela's Central Bank held total reserves of $31 million, but by 1951 these had risen to $373 million. Meanwhile, Venezuela had made much progress from use of oil revenues for economic development, education, and public health. Saudi Arabia, it was urged, would do well to emulate Venezuela's example in this regard, instead of spending all current revenue and borrowing from future revenue.

Most of Saudi Arabia's revenues would be in foreign currencies, mostly dollars, and, as has been mentioned, its foreign exchange transactions had become a major problem. The Agency could help the government to use to best advantage the foreign currencies received. Part would be needed for payments abroad, and part sold for local outlay. Taking over these operations from branches of private foreign banks would bring savings that would justify creating the Agency, apart from anything else.

But the Agency should not unduly curtail the activities which locally established banks and moneychangers might reasonably expect to continue. The Agency could ask the Ka'ki firm to act as its agent in some places where it might not be advisable to establish branches, and thus make use of that firm's experience and organization.

Financial and Economic Research. The government had no machinery for such research. Financial and economic statistics were inadequate or nonexistent. Clearly, the government needed permanent machinery to gather and analyze data to aid in formulating policy. The Agency, therefore, should have a special research department. Such a provision was included in the charter (Article 6).

Operations Not to Be Undertaken. The Agency was to be an important new departure for Saudi Arabia. Over a period of time, the report pointed out, it could be expected to grow and develop new activities under changing conditions as similar institutions in other countries had done. For the present, however, it should begin gradually with the essential functions and gain experience and confidence; and it would not be necessary or expedient to undertake certain activities which similar institutions elsewhere undertook. The charter therefore contained the following provisions (Article 7):

The Agency shall not charge any profits on its receipts and payments and shall not act in any manner which conflicts with the teachings of the Islamic law. The Agency shall not undertake any of the following functions:

(a) Paying or receiving interest.
(b) Receiving private deposits.
(c) Making advances to the Government or to private parties.
(d) Engaging in trade or having an interest in any commercial, industrial or agricultural enterprise.
(e) Buying or holding fixed property except what the Agency reasonably needs for its operations.
(f) Issuing currency notes.

The Agency, said the report, should be a service institution, not operating to seek a profit. It should aim to promote both better operation of the country's monetary system and economy and better administration of the national finances.

In other countries, the report stated, it was the general practice of similar institutions to deal with the public only to the extent necessary to carry out the country's basic monetary policy. Such institutions did not generally accept deposits from the general public or make loans to private parties. The existing commercial banks in Saudi Arabia were in position to supply adequate facilities to the public. The Agency's success, it was stated, would require all possible cooperation from them. This was a further reason why it should not compete with them in receiving deposits, making loans, or buying and selling foreign exchange. The Agency should ordinarily deal only with banks and leave to these the dealings with private parties, whose credit standing and needs they could most readily appraise. The Agency could and should gain the confidence of the banks, and often would be able to help them in their problems.

The Agency should not create credit by issue of currency notes. Saudi Arabia had long been used to metallic money, and under existing conditions it would be wise to continue a "hard-money" system. But this did not mean that Saudi Arabia must forgo the advantages of a convenient means of payment in larger denominations, presently provided by gold, or of elasticity of the supply of money. These advantages could be gained in other ways (see Chapter 7).

The Agency should not make loans to the government. In other countries such loans had been the bane of many similar institutions. If the Agency were to make such loans, these might soon tie up its free funds. Similarly, the Agency should not make loans to private parties. Since the Agency would not receive other than government deposits, it would not have loanable funds apart from the proceeds of public revenues, and these would be needed for the government's use.

In addition, it was clear that the Agency should not engage in trade. It should keep its capital liquid and not tie it up in investments in any commercial, industrial, or agricultural enterprise or by holding fixed property beyond what it reasonably needed for its operations.

The Agency and Economic Development. The report noted that the country's natural resources, except for oil and some other minerals, were quite limited. Therefore, encouragement of economic development was of utmost importance. To an important extent, these resources could be developed and their utilization improved through careful development and better handling of water supply.

Procedure to handle development, it was pointed out, varied in different countries. In some, it was under a board or commission that may include leading officials. In others, special financial institutions had been created to promote development. Also, in some countries development had been handled as a special department of a government bank. The type of procedure best adapted to Saudi Arabia, it was stated, was an important matter for separate determination. But the Agency, even though not itself providing the funds, would be the government's fiscal agent and in position to help in carrying out such plans.

Capital. There were three possibilities with respect to provision of capital: (1) by the government and local financial interests; (2) by the government and a foreign bank; and (3) by the government alone. There was considerable discussion of the first two possibilities and indication that both local and foreign capital might be interested in having a part in the new institution. But Saudi Arabia had no well-developed financial or industrial economy that, as in some countries, would have warranted joint government and private ownership and control. Furthermore, full ownership of the Agency by the government would further its position as strictly a public service institution that should not aim at profit and should be fully divorced from ordinary commercial activities, leaving these to existing private banks. Private interests could be recognized by inclusion of nongovernment members among the directors. Thus, it was concluded that the government should provide the entire capital. The government fully concurred in this conclusion.

It was recommended that the Agency have a capital equivalent to 500,000 sovereigns, calculated at $12 per sovereign and equivalent to $6 million. Since the Agency was not to make loans or receive other than government deposits, it would not need capital to protect the public as creditors. To give the Agency proper standing, both in the country and abroad, and to give elasticity to its operations, it was urged that the greater part of the capital be in liquid funds over and above the initial outlay for buildings and equipment. At least two thirds of the capital should be paid in prior to commencing operations. The government concurred in these proposals. Actually, it paid in cash the entire amount of the capital and provided to the Agency its building at Jidda and equipment without charge to the Agency.

To be assured of sufficient income to cover its expenses, the report stated, the Agency would have to make a reasonable charge to government for services, such as conversion of foreign funds into local currency and transfer of money within the country. Thus, the Agency would be free to act solely on the basis of effectively performing its functions for the benefit of the government and the public. The management would not have to decide the Agency's policy according to whether its operations would be a source of gain.

Direction and Administration. The Agency, it was recommended, should be under control of a board of directors chosen in such manner as to provide for the best practicable consideration of Saudi Arabia's true interests. The minister of finance should be president. The governor of the Agency should be ex officio a member. The board should be a small body with, say, five directors. In August six were named by royal decree: the minister and governor ex officio, the minister's deputy, the vice-governor, and representatives of the Ka'ki firm and the Netherlands Trading Society. Directors, in the wording of Article 33 of the charter of the Reserve Bank of Peru, should be "considered to be representatives of the Nation as a whole, and shall always vote for what they consider to be the general public interest."

Selection of a governor with proper qualifications, the report pointed out, was of utmost importance. The Agency's work would involve many important highly specialized, technical problems. These would include such matters as coinage and issuance of coins and maintenance of their internal and external value; operation of monetary reserve funds; handling foreign exchange transactions so as not to disturb the local market; regulation of commercial banks, foreign exchange dealers, and moneychangers as might be found appropriate; and research to aid the government in determining and carrying out its economic and financial policies.

The government readily accepted my proposal that the first governor be a well-qualified foreign expert who would have charge of the Agency's operations in accordance with its charter and under the general supervision of the board of directors. One of his most important duties, it was pointed out, would be to train a staff of Saudi nationals so that they could gradually assume increasing responsibility with technical competence and in the spirit of public service. Meanwhile, because of the lack of a sufficient number of these, it would be necessary to employ as staff a number of men from other Arab countries, pending the results of a program of training.

INAUGURATION OF THE AGENCY

Once the royal decrees had been issued, it was necessary to provide a suitable building in Jidda, with a vault and other essential equipment; engage the staff both in the country and from abroad; appoint the directors; prepare the bylaws; arrange correspondents abroad; arrange provision of the capital; and determine the initial policies with regard to currency and fiscal agency functions.

Almost any building in Jidda would be available, I was told, for remodeling for the Agency. I was given a free hand to make preparations. The choice was a building of the Finance Ministry with 3-foot-thick walls of coral blocks. A vacant lot adjoining it was the

The Saudi Arabian Monetary Agency, original Jidda building before and after remodeling, 1952 (taken by the author)

site for a connecting vault, which was about 70 feet long, 17 feet wide, and 8.5 feet high. Its walls, floor, and ceiling were built of strongly reinforced concrete 12 inches thick. The vault could hold 30 million silver riyals plus several million gold sovereigns. Construction of the physical arrangements was not easy because of the shortage of skilled labor. Also vault doors and safes had to be ordered from London, which could offer the quickest delivery. As work on the vault had to proceed before these arrived, they had to be lowered into the structure from above. The essential work had been done by the end of summer.

Blowers arrived in Jidda in July and was appointed governor by royal decree as of August 5. As vice-governor, the government appointed Rasim Bey al-Khalidi, a Saudi citizen who had been manager at Jidda for the Arab Bank. To organize the research work and aid with economic problems, the government engaged A. N. McLeod, a Canadian who was with the International Monetary Fund. Blowers engaged staff and arranged for correspondents abroad.

We worked together on preparing the bylaws, arranging with Minister Abd Allah Sulayman both the appointment of directors and prompt provision of the Agency's capital. We also planned the action to be taken to introduce the currency reform when the Agency began operations.

The Agency's opening ceremony on October 4, 1952, was impressive. The heir apparent, Prince Saud, officiated. He arrived in the royal limousine with two uniformed outriders on steps on either side of the car, preceded by two red jeeps loaded with soldiers with submachine guns. Prince Faysal, then minister of foreign affairs, accompanied him. There were brief addresses by the finance minister, the financial adviser, the governor, and a lavish eulogy of Prince Saud delivered by the poet laureate, which was enthusiastically received. After the ceremony the royal party adjourned to inspect the Agency's building. In honor of their visit the rooms were carpeted with splendid rugs borrowed from the palace and were ringed with palace chairs and couches. As the dignitaries left, the thousands who lined the streets cheered.

6

STABILIZING THE WORLD'S HARDEST MONEY

When Abd al-Aziz summoned me to Riyadh before giving the go-ahead for the Monetary Agency, his concern was whether compliance with Islam's tenets was safeguarded. At no time did he ask whether the plan would assure a sound and convenient currency. The Agency's machinery would be there. But the policies followed would show whether the currency's future would be good or bad. For more than a year the Agency managed the currency with no serious difficulty. But the period from the latter part of 1953 through the rest of the 1950s was a time of trouble. Then came years of solid progress.

From the beginning of the financial mission's work, it was clear that serious monetary reform had to wait until the Agency was ready to operate. Meanwhile, analysis of the monetary problems and plans for reform went forward. With the Agency's creation approved, specific action could be planned.

THE MONETARY SYSTEM AND ITS WORKING

From time immemorial Arabia's people, like most others, have been fond of gold and silver coins. In ancient times they used and later copied the money of Byzantium. Arabia itself was long a source of gold and silver. It may have been the site of King Solomon's mines. Tailings abandoned centuries ago were being worked in the early years after World War II by modern methods. Production then averaged about $2 million worth of gold and some silver yearly. Shaykh Abd Allah Sulayman took me to inspect the operation of the Saudi Arabian Mining Syndicate at Mahd al-Dhahab (cradle of gold), about 250 miles from Jidda, where there was talk of expansion with possible government participation. But the operation proved unprofitable and was closed in 1954.[1]

Arabia had a checkered experience with money from the end of World War I to 1952.[2] After the Turks were driven out during the war their money continued in use, along with other foreign coins. Common among these was the old Austrian silver dollar with the image of Queen Maria Theresa, mother of Marie Antoinette. This coin, with dependable silver content, was well known from Arabia and eastern Africa to countries as far away as China. Also, Indian rupees and British gold sovereigns were common.

Before Abd al-Aziz overthrew the Hashimite rule in the Hijaz area, its coins had been used there along with the foreign coins. When he took over that major commercial region in 1926, he first issued cupronickel qirsh coins minted in England. These were needed because of the shortage of small change. The qirsh, whose value was set at 22 to the riyal, ran into trouble, as there were no adequate arrangements to maintain that value in exchange for other currency. Tradesmen and moneychangers imposed on the public by charging unfavorable rates. In 1928 the king issued a riyal coin of the same size and silver content as a former Turkish coin, to be valued at 10 to the British sovereign, then worth $4.8665. But this riyal depreciated as silver prices fell in the depression. In 1936 Abd al-Aziz issued a new silver riyal equal in size and silver content to the Indian rupee. (See Appendix I, Table 5.)

The riyal's value as a full-weight coin was affected by the wide fluctuation of silver prices abroad. From 1936 to 1951 the price in New York ranged between about 45 and 90 cents per ounce. Also beginning in 1949, the riyal's value was affected by the government's placing of very large orders for riyals in England and Mexico. These arrived in lots of 5 million to 10 million and were paid out for payroll and other expenses without regard to maintaining their internal value. Thus in 1949, 60 million were coined; and in 1951 and 1952, 50 million and 77 million were coined, respectively—a total of 187 million. Before 1949 only 98.5 million riyals had been coined. As mentioned in Chapter 3, there was suspicion that profiteering occurred in connection with the issue.

At times riyals so flooded the market that their exchange value fell much below the value of the metal content. In 1949–50 it fell as low as $0.20 while worth over $0.25 abroad (Chart 6.1). That caused extensive smuggling, said to have been 2 million to 5 million riyals monthly for a time. Then, with local supply reduced, the riyal's value

CHART 6.1

Exchange Value of the Riyal at Jidda Compared with Value of Same Weight of Silver at New York and Bombay, 1946–53 *

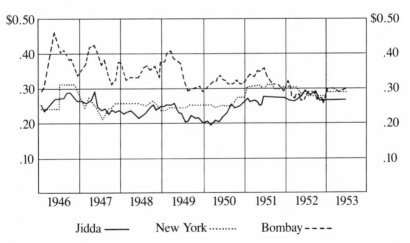

Jidda ——   New York ·········   Bombay - - - -

*Bombay prices are converted to dollars based on the rupee's average value in the free market at Jidda, and are monthly averages except that figures after May 1951 are for mid-month.

SOURCE: Charts 6.1 and 6.2: Arthur N. Young, "Saudi Arabian Currency and Finance," *Middle East Journal*, vol. 7, no. 3 (1953), pp. 364–68.

rose. As of 1951 it was impossible to estimate the quantity of riyals remaining in the country. But it was claimed by some that the defense minister kept an undisclosed large amount, sometimes said to be 15 million or more.

As has been mentioned, for years the British gold sovereign was the chief money for larger transactions in Saudi Arabia. Indian rupee notes were also well known in the eastern region, and, along with other foreign notes, were often seen in the Hijaz area, especially during the pilgrimage. Although the British sovereign was no longer standard money in Britain after it left the gold standard in 1931, it was a widely known coin with dependable gold content. It was recognized all over the world as invaluable for hoarding—a storehouse of value and a protection against inflation. Moreover, it was held for emergencies, especially in countries with unstable political and/or economic conditions.

With the world departing from use of gold coins as standard money, the British sovereign at once began to command a premium compared with the official price, raised in the United States from $20.67 to $35.00 per ounce in 1934. At $35.00 per ounce the sovereign was worth $8.24. But its premium value varied widely in the black, gray, or free markets in many countries. In Jidda from 1946 to 1952 it ranged between $20.00 and $10.25. In 1951–52 the range was between $13.00 and $10.80.

The government had begun receiving Saudi gold sovereigns, minted in Paris on the advice of Christian Delaby. They were practically identical with the British sovereign in weight and fineness (see Appendix I, Table 5). Since, as has been mentioned, the Saudi government was uncertain how best to use them, I recommended waiting for creation of a national bank before deciding.

The combination of worldwide fluctuations in the values of both silver and the old British sovereign made for a wide range of riyal-sovereign rates—between 89.00 and 40.07 from 1946 to 1952. In 1951–52 the range had narrowed but was still large—between 49.32 and 40.07 riyals per sovereign (see Appendix I, Table 4, and Chart 6.2). But the riyal's value in terms of the dollar was held mostly stable from the latter part of 1951, by action later described.

CHART 6.2

Riyal-Sovereign (George Head) Rates at Jidda: Range 1946–53

Riyals per
sovereign

Riyals per
sovereign

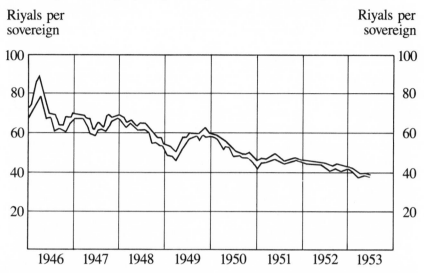

MERITS AND DEFECTS OF THE SYSTEM

Having full-weight metal coins was an element of strength in a world of depreciating paper money. The public had full confidence in the coins. They were durable. They could solidly if not conveniently meet the country's needs. But the defects were serious. Chief of these was instability.

The people suffered from internal fluctuations of the value of the money they held. They had no way of knowing what one coin might be worth in the future in terms of the other. By holding either coin, if they needed the other, they ran the risk of loss, besides paying a commission to a moneychanger or a bank. The only fixed element in the system was the rate between the qirsh and the riyal, 22–1. But that was an odd rate, not easy to compute, and even that rate sometimes varied in times of monetary stringency and despite legal requirements.

The system was also cumbersome. The riyal was a heavy coin in relation to value. For any sizable transaction there was the problem of carrying large weights of metal and counting numbers of coins.

This was troublesome, even though banks and large businesses had mechanical ways to count riyals and stacked them in lots (e.g., lots of one hundred in wooden trays).

Also troublesome was counting gold coins for the larger transactions. Sometimes one would see on the floor of a shop a pile of gold sovereigns being counted, then sorted to separate those with Queen Victoria's image from those with King Edward and King George heads. The latter were at a small premium because, being issued later, they were less worn from handling—not because the man's head was preferred. This exposure of valuable money was quite safe as thievery was almost unknown; a theft might risk loss of a hand, as has been mentioned.

Frequent changes in the foreign exchange value of gold and silver money brought to foreign trade an element of risk and uncertainty. In many countries importers and exporters commonly settle with banks their rates of foreign exchange in advance. Thus, they know its cost or proceeds in local currency. But in Saudi Arabia such forward exchange transactions were almost nonexistent. This was partly because of the interpretation of religious law with regard to any kind of behavior that sought to provide for future contingencies.

To compensate for exchange risks, traders had to allow larger profit margins. They passed on this added cost to the public or the government (as a buyer of imports) in the form of higher prices. This extra burden on trade reduced imports and customs revenue. Finally, by reducing the supply of imported goods, it lowered the standard of living of the people as a whole.

Unstable rates were also disturbing to government finance. About four fifths of the revenue was in foreign currencies, mainly dollars. A large part of this revenue had to be converted into riyals and sovereigns. The government could not budget with assurance when it could not know from month to month what its revenues would be in terms of local currency. The number of riyals realized per dollar had varied from about 3.2 to 5.2 from 1945 to 1951. This meant that the outturn of $1 million ranged from 3.2 million to 5.2 million riyals. With the gold sovereign ranging between $10.25 and $21.00, the outturn of $1 million varied roughly between about 50,000 and 100,000 sovereigns. Even in 1951 the outturn ranged from about

3,550,000 to 4 million riyals, or from about 77,000 to 85,000 sovereigns.

Saudi Arabia needed a revised monetary system. It needed to have a stable standard, with convenient coins of fixed decimal values and freely interchangeable at the holder's wish.

WHAT MONETARY STANDARD?

Soon after my arrival I pointed out to Finance Minister Abd Allah Sulayman that a convenient and stable system could not be based upon full-weight silver and gold coins, owing to the wide fluctuations in worldwide markets. Nor could it be based upon the fluctuating British gold sovereign. Experience had shown that efforts to link the riyal to that coin at a fixed rate were bound to fail.

In 1951–52 the options for choice of a monetary standard were limited. Because of the riyal's great popularity, adopting a silver standard would have been the easiest thing to do. But that would not have been wise. No country was then on a silver standard, though Saudi Arabia with its full-weight riyal was closely related to it. The rest of the world had abandoned that standard during the previous sixty years, and silver's use for coinage was declining. No present or prospective national or international policies gave confidence in silver's future stability. For some time silver prices had been in a narrow range. But in the past they had been highly unstable. A link to silver would lead, sooner or later, to serious difficulties for the public. And the government, with most income in dollars and other foreign currencies, could not know what these would yield in local currency.

To base the currency on gold at the United States official price of $35 per ounce was not practicable. The International Monetary Fund had recently allowed gold producers to sell at a higher price, and there was a premium market for raw gold. Thus, to put out the Saudi gold sovereign at the official price would only feed that market. And to base the monetary system on that sovereign issued at a premium value would be to face a future full of risks.

Clearly, the riyal should be the basis of a reformed system. An ideal reform would have been based on a riyal with less silver content. That would protect against export or melting for commercial use. The Monetary Agency, with a great flow of foreign currencies from oil revenue, could readily maintain such a riyal's value given an adequate reserve. That would mean limiting the supply to actual needs of the public and making riyals convertible on demand into foreign currencies at stable rates. But I was told repeatedly that there were religious objections to a riyal with less than full silver content. That principle had been overlooked, however, when cupronickel qirsh coins were issued in 1946–47.

For money of higher value than the riyal a usual practice would have been for the Monetary Agency to issue paper notes. Some said there were religious objections to that also. But the real problem was doubt about its assurance of value compared with hard money. Furthermore, I had concluded that the Agency's charter should forbid this. The government's record of prodigal spending and poor credit was not encouraging. Even with rapidly growing revenues, then more than twenty times those before the war, it was discounting future receipts from oil. My fears about paper money were to prove correct a few years later.

I found the clue to an improved monetary system in the prospect that the price of silver might be fairly stable for some time. The American Treasury, as a subsidy to the politically powerful silver producers, stood ready in 1951–52 to buy American silver at 90.5 cents per fine ounce.* That price seemed likely to be a ceiling for a good period of time, as the Treasury had announced that it was ready

---

*For decades interests in the American western silver-producing states, despite their small population, took advantage of having two senators each to gain large favors from Washington at the country's expense. The monetary damages thus caused to the United States in the nineteenth century are a matter of history. In the 1930s the American silver buying, besides its cost to the American taxpayer, caused enormous loss and suffering to China, with which I had to cope as financial adviser. That buying drained away much of China's monetary reserves. It acutely aggravated the effects in China of the worldwide depression. It forced adoption of a managed paper currency as the only practicable solution. This currency was sound for some time, but the outbreak of the Sino-Japanese war in 1937 forced China to rely heavily upon paper-money financing. This led to the great wartime and postwar inflation that had a part in changing China's history.

Particulars of the China experience are given in my two books: *China's Nation-Building Effort, 1927–1937* (Stanford, Calif.: Hoover Institution Press, 1971), and *China's Wartime Finance and Inflation, 1937–1945* (Cambridge, Mass.: Harvard University Press, 1965).

to sell some 160 million ounces at that level. Thus, the riyal could be given an exchange value that would protect it from export, so that the price abroad would have to rise well above 90.5 cents to justify the costs of export.

A drop in the world silver price need not be serious. The demand for riyals would continue strong as the country developed. New coins were being absorbed at the rate of 30 million or more yearly. The Agency would not need large reserves to enable it to withdraw riyals from the public by converting them to foreign currencies at par on demand if they became redundant.

Since the full-weight silver riyal had to be central to any monetary reform, it was my good fortune to be in Saudi Arabia when conditions made it possible to plan a monetary reform based on that coin. The converging of its value and world silver prices is clearly seen in Chart 6.1. Such a reform seemed likely to succeed for some time. Actually it was 1961 before the world silver price rose much or for long above 90.5 cents.[3] Also, there was hope that in case of such a rise, changing views as modernization proceeded would allow a riyal with less silver. After all, minor fiduciary coins had been issued.

TEMPORARY STABILIZATION

In the latter part of 1951, pending a decision about a national bank, I arranged with Finance Minister Abd Allah Sulayman to begin a temporary stabilization of the riyal-dollar exchange rate. I pointed out to him the disastrous result in 1949–50 of paying out riyals without regard to their internal and external value (Chart 6.1). He agreed to my proposal to control the issue of riyals. The existing stock on hand, plus newly minted coins to be impounded upon arrival, would be paid out with regard to maintaining the riyal's exchange value. Thus, riyals would be released only when the riyal's exchange value tended to rise. Conversely, when it tended to fall, the ministry was to anticipate Treasury requirements by buying riyals in the market.

Thus, an informal stabilization was effected, beginning in the latter part of 1951. Rates were held within a fairly narrow range from then until the Monetary Agency opened in October 1952, except that during the summer some temporary appreciation of the riyal took place.

The season of the pilgrimage then came in the summer. We foresaw that we would have to issue more riyals, both to meet the added needs of business when the pilgrims came and to prevent a rise in the riyal's foreign exchange value. For several reasons this need was not duly met. Newly ordered riyals did not arrive in time. I was out of the country for two weeks to recuperate from illness, and Najib Bey Salihah did not pay out available riyals on hand (he left for good suddenly the day after my return).[4] Shaykh Abd Allah was away, so there was no one to act. Also, in 1952 there was less than usual use of Indian rupee notes, whose use the government had restricted in 1951, and of Egyptian notes which were less used because of the uncertain political situation in Egypt.

Besides the problem about silver, there was still the question as to what to do about issuing the 2 million Saudi gold sovereigns which had been ordered on Delaby's recommendation. What should be their relation to the riyal? Soon after I arrived, I told Shaykh Abd Allah that Delaby's plan of issuing them at 40–1 did not then appear feasible. But by the fall of 1952 most of them had arrived and the government wanted to use them. Conditions had changed, with the Monetary Agency about to be in position to deal with currency matters. The gold was on the books at the par value of about $8.24 at $35.00 per ounce. The free market price was $37.00 to $38.00 in September 1952—a far cry from gold prices today. The British sovereign in that month averaged $12.10 at Jidda. At a 27-cent value for the riyal, the Saudi sovereign at 40–1 would be worth $10.80. If the government accepted it for all payments due it, and if the Agency would redeem it on demand for 40 riyals, issuance of the 2 million gold sovereigns seemed feasible. In any event, issuance would not risk loss to the government.

This would be a new development in monetary matters—a fiduciary gold coin. But it would have to be made clear that maintaining its value, as in the case of the riyal, would be subject to changes in the world prices of gold and silver.

THE REFORM OF OCTOBER 1952

The key to monetary reform was choosing the right level for stabilizing the riyal. This had to be done with great care, to cause the least possible disturbance. I found no reason why the level should not be close to the fairly stable rates of the recent past, to which the public was accustomed and to which the economy was adjusted. Also, the riyal should not be given a value so low that it would be profitable to export coins as silver. It had 0.34375 oz. of pure silver, worth about 31 cents if silver were at 90.5. The margin of safety against smuggling out was about 15 percent, to cover costs and the average lighter weight of used and worn coins. Hence, the rate should not be much below 27 cents.

During the summer, while the Monetary Agency's building was being prepared, I was ill. Since Blowers had arrived and could supervise the preparations, I could leave the heat of Jidda with Mrs. Young to regain strength. I said I wanted to go to Greece so I would be able to consult the oracle at Delphi as to what the rate of exchange should be. On my return after visiting Delphi I reported that the oracle said: "Not too high, not too low"!

As the opening of the Monetary Agency drew nearer, important decisions were needed. Besides plans for setting up the Agency, there were the day-to-day operations to keep the riyal as stable as possible, choice of the riyal's exchange value, the eventual program to stabilize it, and what to do with the Saudi gold sovereign. Thus, Blowers and I had much to discuss with Shaykh Abd Allah Sulayman.

In the year to mid-1952 the riyal had fortunately been unusually steady at about 27 cents or 3.7 to the dollar. The equilibrium was such that few stabilization operations were needed. The rise during the pilgrimage to about 28.5 cents was not checked for the reasons stated. With the pilgrimage ended, demand for riyals would slacken. Also, newly coined riyals had arrived. For these reasons a rate lower than 28.50 cents was indicated.

Fortunately also, the situation in the silver market was favorable to a rate around 27 cents. In 1952 the New York price ranged only between 82.75 and 88 cents. From July 24 to October 1 it had been steady at around 83 cents, equivalent to a bullion parity of 28.50 cents for the riyal. Also, at that price the riyal's value as bullion was about the same as its value in New York and Bombay, an unusual condition. (See Chart 6.1).

I concluded that a rate lower than about 26.75 was inadvisable, because of the risk of smuggling if silver rose to around 90.50 cents

or more in New York. The rate should not be above the recent level
of 28.50, which seemed likely to be a temporary condition. Assuming a full-weight riyal, the Agency could base its immediate policy,
but without commitment for the future, on a price range for silver
between about 80 and 90.50 cents. Actually, the price did not rise
much or for long above the 80-cent to 90.50-cent range until it rose
above $1.00 in 1961.

Blowers concurred in my recommending to Shaykh Abd Allah that
the Agency should begin by stabilizing the riyal at between 26.75
and 27.50 cents, subject of course to changes in the value of silver.
That level also would give the government a satisfactory outturn from
conversion of foreign currencies to riyals. After some discussion
Shaykh Abd Allah agreed.

I repeatedly stressed to him that exchange stability of a full-weight
silver riyal could not be assured indefinitely. The ultimate solution
was a riyal with less silver, to be held firmly at a fixed value. Also,
I urged this at my last meeting with the heir apparent, Prince Saud,
when he raised no objection. But the government was not ready to
take this step.

There remained the problem of the Saudi gold sovereign, which
the government was anxious to issue. As noted earlier, it was worth
$8.24 at $35.00 per ounce, but at the free gold price in the fall of
1952 its value was $8.70 to $8.95. At such a level the coin would
be drained away to black, gray, or free markets or melted down (e.g.,
for jewelry).

As a new and unproved coin, it was best for it to be issued at a
value lower than the popular and well-established British sovereign.
A possible rate of 40–1 for riyals had long been discussed. With the
riyal at 26.75 or 27.50 cents, a 40–1 rate would give a value of
$10.70 to $11.00. In September the widely known British sovereign
was worth a little over $12.00 in Jidda. Of course, any fixed rate
should be subject to change if required by changes in the world markets for gold or silver. With 2 million sovereigns, conversion into
riyals could be guaranteed. After determining acceptability of the new
coin, a lesser reserve of riyals might be possible. Furthermore, acceptance of the Saudi sovereign in all payments to the government
would encourage its favorable reception by the public. Since the sov-

ereigns were on the government's books at $35.00 per ounce plus expenses, it did not stand to lose on issuance at 40–1.

The Monetary Agency opened on October 4, 1952. Prior to its opening Shaykh Abd Allah called a meeting of the bankers and leading businessmen at which he, Blowers, and I explained at length the Agency's work and the program of currency reform. At once the Agency began operations to lower foreign exchange rates for the riyal from the relatively high level obtaining since June 1952, to a figure in line with the average rates that prevailed in the preceding eighteen months. It issued newly coined riyals arriving from Mexico and aggressively bought dollars. Its action was promptly effective, aided by the cooperation of local banks and money dealers. On October 4 the riyal quotation was $0.2857. By October 22 it had fallen to $0.2725.

At that level the time had come to announce issuance of the Saudi gold sovereign. With the riyal at $0.2725, the sovereign's value at 40–1 would be $10.90. Minister Abd Allah Sulayman, in announcing the 40–1 rate on October 22, stated that the Agency would "operate in the market with banks and authorized money dealers to prevent fluctuations in rates of foreign exchange." The Agency, he said, "will maintain these rates unless prevented by major changes in the world prices of gold or silver." All government departments would accept sovereigns at 40–1 vis-à-vis riyals. Export of Saudi sovereigns was forbidden, with a reward to informers of a fourth of the value of sovereigns seized from smugglers. British sovereigns and other gold coins could be exported freely, subject to customs regulations and licensing by the Agency.

The minister further announced creation of a Currency Reserve Fund, which would include the amounts by which sovereigns exceeded their cost, and that the size of the fund would be increased. (Unfortunately, the latter did not happen.) The fund also would include nearly $5 million available under an agreement with the United States. That represented the dollar proceeds of silver lend-leased to Saudi Arabia during World War II.

With the Monetary Agency working well, the currency reform successfully begun, an improved tariff and better customs procedures close to adoption, and work on matters of budget and accounting well under way, I could feel comfortable in leaving for the United States.

Under the date of October 19 I submitted to Shaykh Abd Allah a report of fifty-three pages including statistical annexes, reviewing the work, explaining the reasons for the reforms, and suggesting future financial policies. I stressed the need for a riyal with less silver, to protect against the effects of a possible rise in silver prices. I also proposed adjusting the qirsh to 25 per riyal (later a rate of 20 was adopted, which I think was better).

The reforms adopted were not perfect, and the uncertainties about the future of the riyal and sovereign were clear. But, especially with the creation of the Monetary Agency, a foundation for progress had been laid. How it would be built upon was in the hands of Allah.

CONCLUSION OF A MISSION

On the eve of my departure Shaykh Abd Allah gave me a dinner, inviting the members of the diplomatic corps and leaders of the Saudi and foreign business community. It was pleasant to be with many who had become friends, but with a touch of sadness that I would see few of them again. Shaykh Abd Allah was gracious enough to praise my work, especially the help I gave in establishing the Monetary Agency. In response I thanked him for so effectively working for reforms, recognized the helpful cooperation of other officials and of business leaders, and in particular expressed appreciation of the interest and support of His Majesty King Abd al-Aziz and His Royal Highness Prince Saud. The success attained, I said, had been made possible because of these factors and because the time was ripe for adoption of financial reforms, and not merely because of what I had done.

Apropos of this, Ambassador Ray Hare wrote a letter, from which I quote:

I recall that, at the time of your arrival here, I told you of the interest of the American Government, as a friend of Saudi Arabia, in doing what it could to contribute to the financial stability of this country by assisting in the inauguration of appropriate financial practices and administration. I explained that others before you had made efforts along this line but without appreciable success. I emphasized that the task was not only great but delicate, but that I hoped that with your experience in similar endeavors elsewhere you would find a way of rendering effective service. Now it is with great pleasure and satisfaction that we can review the truly unusual progress made during your tour of duty here. Not only did you achieve outstanding success in fostering the setting up of the Monetary Agency and directing others in the fields of budgetary and customs work, but you were able to do so by establishing a legacy of friendship and respect on the part of both your American and Saudi colleagues.

7

THE MONETARY AGENCY
PROVES ITSELF

George Blowers, as the Agency's first governor, deserves high praise for organizing it and keeping the currency stable for the first two years. Then came a period of deterioration, owing to overspending and failure to create adequate currency reserves from the ample revenues from oil. Finally, following the drastic reforms of the late 1950s, directed by then heir apparent, Prince Faysal ibn Abd al-Aziz, and supported by King Saud, Saudi Arabia and the Agency began years of solid growth and achievement.

TROUBLES AND PROGRESS

A problem left for the future in 1952 was how best to have the money supply expand and contract to take care of the bulge of activity at the time of the pilgrimage. Temporary issue of more riyals and sovereigns could help, aided by use of foreign paper money. But a more far-reaching solution, announced on July 23, 1953, was Blowers' decision to issue "pilgrim receipts." This would make it easier for pilgrims to change their foreign currencies into money usable in the country. And it would get around the clause in the Agency's charter that forbade "issuing currency notes." Pilgrim receipts were first issued in denominations of 10, 100, and 1,000 riyals, and later 5 and 1 riyals. Each receipt bore in Arabic and English a statement that the Agency "held in its vaults" the specified number of riyals "at the disposal of the bearer of this fully negotiable receipt."

In the pilgrimage season culminating in August 1953 the Agency issued about 25 million pilgrim receipts. After the pilgrimage only about a fifth came back to the Agency.[1] They soon were generally accepted by the public, thus gaining the status of paper money.

The new Saudi gold sovereign was well received in the Jidda-Mecca area. But it was less readily accepted in Riyadh and the oil area, where gold coins had not been generally used. Aramco, however, had paid oil royalties in British gold sovereigns from the beginning, until it obtained the right to pay in foreign currencies. After the Saudi gold sovereign was issued, Aramco cooperated to promote acceptance of the new coin and protection of its value. Countrywide the demand by the summer of 1953 was such that most of the 2 million sovereigns had been put in circulation.

But in the latter part of 1953 counterfeits began to appear, mostly with full gold content. This was a surprise, as there had been little counterfeiting of the British sovereign. The shock to confidence caused a run on the Monetary Agency to redeem Saudi sovereigns in riyals. By early 1954 about three fourths of the sovereigns had been redeemed. Then the call for redemption slackened. A sovereign of a different design was issued later. But Saudi sovereigns did not become a major part of the currency and were demonetized in 1959.[2] Having been put out at a value well above the official gold price, their issuance had caused no loss.

The Agency's redemption of sovereigns during 1953–54 enhanced public confidence in the currency. Having pilgrim receipts on hand helped to meet the demand for redemption, although the Agency paid them out only when specifically requested. The issue of pilgrim receipts fell to about 10 million riyals late in 1953. But the convenience of their use soon led to increase to nearly 30 million.[3] Nevertheless, the redemption of sovereigns left the Agency with an excess of sovereigns and less liquid. It was less able to maintain the value of riyals and sovereigns because the government, despite the large flow of oil revenue, had not strengthened the Agency's reserves of foreign currencies—action that I had repeatedly urged to be necessary.

King Abd al-Aziz died late in 1953 and was widely mourned as a great leader. His eldest living son, Saud ibn Abd al-Aziz succeeded him. Saud had told me at Riyadh of his dislike for Shaykh Abd Allah Sulayman; and he replaced him as finance minister with his deputy, Muhammad Surur. Also, Blowers left in 1954 when his two-year contract ended. R. D. Standish was named governor on his recommendation. He was an experienced American banker but did not have central banking experience, as did his predecessor.

Blowers, who after returning to Washington had become a director of the Export-Import Bank, sent me with a letter of June 20, 1955, the translation of a royal decree amending the Agency's charter. Besides increasing the finance minister's authority in operations, the governor could be appointed or dismissed by the Council of Ministers instead of by royal decree. Other of the Agency's higher officials could be appointed or dismissed by the Council of Ministers, and some officials by the minister.

Blowers said in his letter that ever since he had left, "they have been in the process of taking authority from the Governor bit by bit." He said that before he left he tried to convince Muhammad Surur that "very strong powers in the hands of the Governor could be of great help to him as Minister of Finance but I am afraid I didn't succeed." This was understandable since, once the Monetary Agency was successfully operating, pressure of nationalism limited what a non-Muslim could do in the highly important post of governor. Blowers could not confer on another his mantle of prestige. He felt that the troubles after he left were not Standish's fault.

In 1954 Surur devalued the riyal by 1 percent. He did this the day after Blowers left and without consulting him or Standish.[4] The apparent motive was to increase the return from converting dollars and other foreign currencies into riyals. Surur's move apparently was to help to meet the government's demand for money. A costly program of development was under way, to improve water resources, agriculture, roads, ports, airports, public health, and education. Also, according to a report of the U.S. Department of Commerce, "erection of new palaces in major cities was proceeding at a rapid rate."[5]

Oil revenue grew from $110 million in 1951 to nearly $341 million in 1955. The government counted upon rapid growth to continue indefinitely. But that was not to be. Revenue leveled off: the 1955 figure was not surpassed until 1961. Yet revenues were good, averaging over $300 million yearly through 1960 (see Appendix I, Table 1). Oil prices were often low—at one time as low as $1.24 per barrel. (This was a factor in the creation of OPEC in 1960.) Serious difficulties followed.

Until 1955 the Monetary Agency was able to keep the riyal stable, despite fluctuations in the price of silver. But there was a risk in relying upon a full-weight silver coin—I had failed to convince the government to issue coins with less silver. Even if the riyal were worth a little more as silver than as money, it would not pay to smuggle riyals out so long as the difference stayed less than 10 to 15 percent. So Surur's measure added to the risk of smuggling.

Early in 1955, however, a rise in the price of silver made smuggling profitable. A major cause of the rise was action by Saudi Arabia itself. The price had been remarkably steady at around 85 cents per ounce from January 1953 to March 1955. But early in 1955, apparently either without consulting Standish or taking his advice, Saudi Arabia ordered 50 million riyals (17.2 million ounces). These were to be supplied and minted in Mexico.

This big order, along with other demands, reduced Mexico's stock of silver to only 11 million ounces. On March 11 the Bank of Mexico announced that it had no more silver for sale. Meanwhile, the American Treasury's free stocks, which had been 160 million ounces at the end of 1950, had fallen to 13.6 million ounces at the end of 1954. Larger demand and smaller supply caused the silver price to rise above 90 cents. It stayed between 90 and 92 cents for most of the rest of 1955 and during 1956.[6]

The size of the order for riyals was a serious blunder. It suggests that someone profited from the deal, as in the case of earlier orders. And Surur's 1 percent devaluation in 1954 made matters worse. It was no surprise, therefore, that the higher price of silver caused a heavy drain of full-weight silver riyals from Saudi Arabia. In 1955 and 1956 more than 18 million riyals were shipped to New York. And there were further shipments to other centers.[7]

The Monetary Agency could have handled the problems for some time, given adequate reserves and proper policies. After briefly reaching 92 cents in 1955, the silver price did not exceed 91.625 cents until 1961. Part of this time it was 1 to 3 cents lower.[8] Even after Surur's devaluation, either no riyals or fewer could have been ordered, thus avoiding or lessening pressure on silver. Oil revenues in 1954 and 1955 were $236.3 million and $340.8 million, respectively. Only a small part of these could have provided adequate reserves. As to policies, the Agency could have prevented a fall in the riyal's exchange value by avoiding overissue of new coins and redeeming them on demand. Pilgrim receipts, properly controlled and freely redeemable in foreign exchange at par, could have replaced riyals if export developed.

Meanwhile, the Monetary Agency added to the difficulties by beginning to make loans to the government, an inflationary practice that has caused so much grief to the world. The charter of 1952 expressly forbade loans to the government or to private parties (see Appendix III, Article 7c). According to the Agency's first annual report, for 1960–61,

The Government deficits were financed both by internal borrowing, mainly from the Monetary Agency, and external loans. . . . Net indebtedness to the Monetary Agency alone amounted to about Rls. 700 million [about $150 million] by the middle of 1377 [early 1958].[9]

This report was presented on behalf of the board of directors by Anwar Ali who, as told later, became governor in 1958.

During 1955 pilgrim receipts began to go to a discount in foreign exchange. By early 1956 the free rate for notes was about 4.00 per dollar, a discount of about 6 percent, and by the end of the year the rate was about 4.40 per dollar. Despite efforts to control imports and the export of capital, the riyal's free market value fluctuated widely and continued to fall. In the first half of 1958 it ranged from about 5.20 to 6.25 per dollar. Meanwhile, note reserves of gold, silver, and foreign currencies fell to only 14 percent.[10]

In the spring of 1958 the government adopted important reforms that effectively checked the deterioration of the finances. Prince Faysal was the prime mover in the reforms, in which King Saud cooperated. Spending for "Royal Palaces and Princes" had grown from 36 million riyals in the budget for 1952–53 to 236 million in 1959 for the "Private Treasury." Allowing for exchange depreciation the increase was four- or fivefold. For the next few years such spending was stabilized at about the 1959 level. It was cut by about one fourth after Prince Faysal succeeded Saud as king in 1964.[11]

Spending for projects of development and other postponable purposes was also drastically cut. Large payments were made on internal and external debt. Luxury imports were discouraged, and import of automobiles was temporarily banned. Currency reserves were increased from 14 percent in mid-1958 to 100 percent at the end of 1959. The riyal's exchange value gradually improved to about 4.5 per dollar.

Saudi Arabia joined the International Monetary Fund in August 1957. Thus, the fund, which has an outstanding record in helping members with troubled finances, was able to aid in reforms. In 1958 Saudi Arabia appointed Anwar Ali as governor of the Monetary Agency. He was a highly qualified Pakistani who had been an expert of the fund. He played an important part in helping to restore the finances.

With a background of solid improvement, the government announced a definitive monetary reform on December 31, 1959. It fixed the riyal at a gold par equal to 4.5 per dollar, in line with its recent value, and made it freely convertible. It divided the riyal into 20 instead of the inconvenient 22 qirsh. Controls of trade and exchange were ended. Saudi gold sovereigns were to be redeemed at the par of 40–1 for two months. Then the sovereigns and silver riyals were to become only commodities. Pilgrim receipts were abolished, and in their place notes backed by 100 percent reserve were issued. By the end of 1959 reserves were $186 million, compared with $24 million two years earlier. The Monetary Agency was given a new charter, authorizing it to become a full-fledged central bank.

After the years of growing pains the reforms of 1959 restored confidence at home and abroad. They cleared the way for more progress.

Credit for these reforms is due primarily to Prince Faysal, who saw the need for firm action and won the support of King Saud, and of course to Anwar Ali, whose technical and administrative skills were essential.

THE MONETARY AGENCY BECOMES A FINANCIAL POWER

Governor Anwar Ali presented the Agency's first annual report for 1960–61. It contained 23 pages of text dealing in detail with financial and economic events, together with 40 pages of statistical tables. The series of annual reports that followed has maintained the high standards of that report, and gradually increased the analyses and statistical coverage. The report for 1981 had 106 pages of text and 72 pages of tables. Soon after beginning the annual reports the Agency began a *Statistical Summary*. It was issued twice yearly from 1969, with the same high standards as the reports. These documents contain full data of Saudi Arabia's financial and economic history. Their content and form would be a credit to any country. The Agency's Research Department has come a long way from the time when I had my Lebanese assistant go to Jidda's *suq* twice weekly to gather data about prices.

Anwar Ali's first annual report described the troubles of the middle 1950s and how they were overcome. It said that the Agency could "take justifiable satisfaction in its role in smoothing the transition and bringing about the present favorable economic climate." The situation had been stabilized, he said, but "the task of development has just begun," bringing "a new set of problems." The government, he believed, was "pursuing appropriate policies" of development which he expected would "bring greater prosperity to people at large" (page 23).

Anwar Ali, after helping to bring about the urgently needed reforms of 1957–60, presided effectively over the Agency's later progress. I kept in touch with him; he said that the first thing he read when asked to work on Saudi problems was my report on establishing the Monetary Agency (see Appendix II). He arranged for the Agency to send me copies of its publications as issued. Credit also should go to Finance Minister Prince Musa'id ibn Abd al-Rahman, brother of his late majesty, King Faysal, for his effective work during the 1960s and until 1976.

Basically the responsibility for constructive change was that of Prince Faysal ibn Abd al-Aziz. He kept a firm hand on the working of the reforms and the process of modernization. But as King Saud's problems mounted and his health was poor, the Council of Princes decided that Faysal should replace him as king. Faysal demurred; he had sworn allegiance to Saud. His regard for traditional values was shown by a reported incident at Riyadh in 1948. He was returning from a UN meeting in New York that he had attended as foreign minister. Saud, his elder brother and heir apparent met him. When they were being driven from the airport Saud sat on the back seat and Faysal sat on the floor at his feet.[12] Finally in 1964 Faysal reluctantly agreed to become king. He saw that it was necessary for the country's good. He was assassinated by a deranged relative in 1975.

Anwar Ali died on June 22, 1974, soon after signing the Agency's annual report for 1973–74, and Abd al-Aziz al-Qurayshi became governor. It was a landmark that a Saudi national took this significant post.

The riyal was kept stable vis-à-vis the dollar for a decade, until the dollar departed from gold in 1971. Then the riyal's value fluctuated upward from 4.5 to around 3.5 to the dollar. As of March 15, 1975, Saudi Arabia chose to link to the "basket" of leading currencies represented by the special drawing rights (SDR) of the International Monetary Fund.* The link was at a parity of 4.28255 riyals per SDR, with a band of 7.25 percent on either side.[13] In December 1981 the riyal's dollar equivalent was around 30 cents, strikingly not far from the level of 27.25 cents set in 1952.

Started with capital equal to only $6 million, the Agency has since become one of the world's most important financial institutions. Its first statement of condition as of March 16, 1953, showed total assets of 59.4 million riyals, or about $15 million. As of September 30, 1981, it held foreign assets equivalent to $119 billion, not including

*Special drawing rights (SDR) represent the average of exchange rates of the American, British, French, German, and Japanese currencies. During 1981 the value of the SDR ranged between about $1.10 and $1.25.

The Saudi Arabian Monetary Agency, headquarters office, 1982 (courtesy of the Saudi Arabian Monetary Agency)

4,567,000 ounces of Saudi gold. With such assets Saudi Arabia ranks high among the world's countries as a holder of international assets.[14]

Governor al-Qurayshi, in the Agency's annual report of 1977, summarized the monetary events of the first twenty-five years of its history and their significance. The riyal had become "one of the strongest currencies in the world," although it weakened internally in the 1970s because of rapidly rising world prices and the pressure of unprecedented domestic spending. The tremendous growth in the demands on the Agency as the government's fiscal agent is shown by 147-fold increase of the budget since it was created. That followed an increase from about $7 million in the 1930s before oil revenue began, to the equivalent of $205 million in 1952–53. For the 1970s, said the governor, the challenges arose "from an inflow of financial resources that had been faster and larger than the country was physically equipped to absorb." But he felt "reassured that the country will be able to respond successfully to the challenges it is facing." [15]

It is gratifying to look back on the Agency's constructive part in events since its founding. It has developed and expanded the basic functions set out in the 1952 charter, along with the country's growing strength and the ability of its leaders to manage the finances. It has discharged well the arduous task of managing the vast income and assets at home and abroad. From the start it has had to convert huge receipts, nearly all in foreign currencies, into the riyals needed. It has been able to minimize the inflationary effects of the buildup of huge reserves abroad. It has had a key part in operation of the national budget, with the huge spending for development. There are clearing-house operations for checks. It regulates the commercial banks, which cover the country with numerous branches. Its research and statistical work is of high quality, reflected in excellent annual reports and semiyearly *Statistical Summaries*.

I venture to quote two comments. Parker T. (Pete) Hart, who was American Ambassador to Saudi Arabia during the years 1961–65 (after the reforms of 1958–59), wrote to me that the Monetary Agency had "certainly kept that country on a sound financial footing, a source of stability and pride to Saudi Arabia and an example for the entire area." And Tom Barger, who in posts of high responsibility has watched Saudi Arabia's changing scene since the early days of oil, has written to me that by the autumn of 1952 the "essential elements" of the foundations for the country's financial institutions "were in place, and . . . so well designed that they survived the troubles of King Saud's reign, provided the means for King Faysal to restore the financial soundness of the Kingdom and so flexible that they exist today when the daily revenue of the Kingdom matches the annual revenue of 1952." That, he said, could not have been "wrought so well without the participation and backing of the Saudis themselves."

8

OVERVIEW: AN EVENTFUL HALF CENTURY, 1932–82

Saudi Arabia has changed quite spectacularly in the fifty years since King Abd al-Aziz proclaimed the Kingdom of Saudi Arabia in 1932. He, the successive rulers, and their people have transformed the country from a little-known desert land into one of the world's key countries, in both economic and international affairs. Its policy concerning oil is a basic factor in the world economy; it imports foreign goods and services on a large scale; and its huge assets abroad make it important in international finance. It provides large aid to developing countries, both directly and through Arab, Islamic, and other international agencies, including the International Monetary Fund and the World Bank.

Not only do oil and financial strength make Saudi Arabia important. Its exposed position in the troubled area of the Middle East and Indian Ocean makes its security and foreign policy crucial for its own future and for world order and peace. Altogether, its resources, strategic location, position in the Arab and Islamic world, and active foreign policy make it a country to be reckoned with.

Let us look broadly at these aspects.

THE OIL BONANZA

The fantastic growth of Saudi Arabia's revenue since income from oil began suggests comparison with the tales of the genie in *Arabian Nights*. In only about forty years total revenue has grown about 17,000-fold: from about $7 million in the late 1930s to $118.7 billion, including $108.9 billion from oil (preliminary) in its fiscal year ended May 4, 1981. At that rate, a single day's oil revenue is much more than the entire yield of $212.2 million in 1952, when the Monetary Agency was founded.[1]

Growth of oil revenue had four phases:

1. increase of oil production from 1945, after having been held back because of World War II
2. increase of the government's share of profits to 50 percent from January 1, 1951
3. larger production of oil after 1960, reflecting new discoveries and growing world demand
4. the huge increases of prices by OPEC after the oil embargo imposed in late 1973

Oil revenue first reached $1 billion yearly in 1970. Then began the astronomical growth. In 1973 it reached $4.3 billion; the oil embargo ran from October to early 1974. In that year it spurted to $22.6 billion, before almost quadrupling by 1980–81. The growth is shown in Chart 8.1. Nonoil revenue has been of the order of 10 percent of growing total revenue in recent years, largely reflecting growth of income from investments abroad.[2] In 1980–81 the total revenue of Saudi Arabia, with its few million people, was about one sixth of that of the United States with its population of more than 200 million.

The huge flow of money provided ample reserves and investments abroad as noted in Chapter 7. The currency had been wrecked temporarily in the 1950s by overspending and failure to set aside proper reserves. But the lesson was learned, and reserves have since been adequate. Reserves minus gold were $32.2 billion as of December 31, 1981, exceeded only by Germany's $43.7 billion. The United States had $18.9 billion. As to gold, Saudi Arabia showed holdings of 4.567 million ounces—about 3 million ounces were shown from

CHART 8.1
Oil Revenue, 1938–81
(semilogarithmic scale)

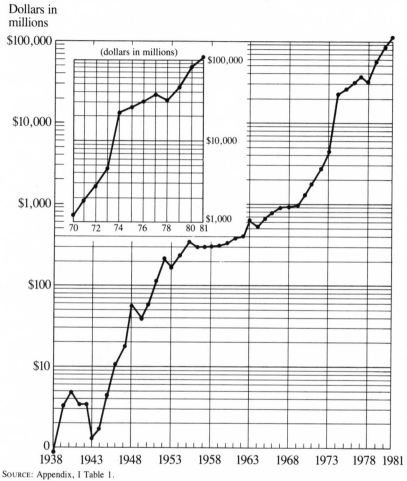

Dollars in
millions

SOURCE: Appendix, I Table 1.

1972 until mid-1978.[3] The other two countries showed much larger gold holdings, especially the United States.

Saudi Arabia has large holdings of American Treasury securities and certificates of deposit in American banks. There are also lesser investments in bonds and equities of leading American corporations.

There are also holdings of Eurodollars and investments in countries other than the United States, including notably Germany and Japan. Holdings abroad are not published. In financial circles they were estimated to be of the order of $160 billion to $180 billion as of early 1982.[4] Saudi nationals who have benefitted from economic expansion also have large holdings abroad, and presumably some hold gold.

Oil revenue also made possible the largest spending program in history to develop a country's economy and human resources. In the 1950s spending for development was only tens of millions of dollars yearly. The big increase of spending began after oil revenue reached $1 billion in 1970. The phenomenal spending that is transforming Saudi Arabia was made possible by the burgeoning of oil revenue under OPEC's policies following the oil embargo of 1973. Spending for all purposes rose from $1.4 billion in 1970–71 to $70.6 billion ten years later. The major part of this was for development (see Appendix I, Table 9).

THE ECONOMIC AND SOCIAL UNDERPINNING

Growing financial strength needs to be supported by a growing economy, with a people able to operate it successfully. More and more the leaders recognize this. They know that oil reserves will eventually shrink, and they want the country to be prepared. That means having greater and more diversified resources, both material and human. To discuss this in depth would take us too far afield. But a brief summary will help to complement the financial side.

Never has a country's overall situation been transformed as rapidly and drastically as that of Saudi Arabia in the past half century. King Abd al-Aziz was strictly loyal to Islam and its tenets, having inherited the rigorous Wahhabi tradition. Yet he saw that the country had to modernize.

Serious development began in the 1930s, with water and agriculture. By 1952, as oil revenue grew, the cost of public projects completed, under way, and planned was about $354 million. These included water and electrical projects for the main cities, roads, airports, and the railway from the oil area to Riyadh.[5]

After Amir Saud succeeded Abd al-Aziz as king in 1953, overspending, which had gone on for some time, led to the financial troubles noted in Chapter 7. After Prince Faysal intervened in the late 1950s to restore order, development projects continued actively but with regard for financial capacity.

The development plans from 1971 were worked out with the help of the United States–Saudi Arabian Joint Commission on Economic Cooperation. The plans seek progress while maintaining the religious and moral values of Islam. The First Development Plan, from 1971 to 1974, began after oil revenue reached $1 billion in 1970. Budgeted for about $16 billion, it cost about $20 billion. Major items were for transport and communications; port improvement and new ports; agriculture and water resources, including more plants to desalinize seawater; and creation of industries based on petrochemicals and minerals. The plan also included items for education, social development, and defense.

When income from oil leaped ahead to $22.6 billion in 1974, the much greater Second Development Plan, for 1975–80, became possible. Its goal was to develop and diversify the economy; develop human resources by education, training, and health improvement; and assure the kingdom's security and social stability. Budgeted for $141.5 billion, it cost about $200 billion. It largely put in place the basic structure of communications and power.[6]

The Third Development Plan, running to 1985, continued what went before.[7] Its estimated cost was $285 billion but may well be greater. It aimed to reduce dependence on oil as the main revenue source. It provided for maintenance of buildings, roads, ports, airports, schools, and hospitals. It stressed aid for a variety of light and labor-intensive industrial businesses, which it hoped would develop in the private sector. It gave great weight to large enterprises such as petrochemicals. To help with the program, it offered encouragement by favorable treatment by customs exemption, and in taxation, supply of sites, housing, power, and water. It continued development of large projects, oil-related and others, jointly with major foreign firms. Two new sites were being developed from scratch, expecting tens of thousands of residents: al-Jubayl on the Persian-Arabian Gulf for petrochemicals, a steelmill, and other industries, and Yanbu' on the Red Sea. Yanbu' has become an important oil terminal, with a pipeline from the oilfields opened in mid-1981 whose capacity of 1,850,000 barrels per day (bpd) could be doubled. Flaring of gas wells, formerly a spectacular sight, was being ended with the gas used for power and to produce gasoline and propane.

A major project was direct investment of the Saudi government in the oil industry. Its oil company is Petromin (General Petroleum and Minerals Organization). Petromin is increasingly active in many phases of oil-related enterprises and wants to expand more broadly in the oil business. Also, the government has invested directly by buying substantially all Aramco's assets in Saudi Arabia. Purchase began with 25 percent in 1972 and later increased to 60 percent. Transfer was mostly completed in 1980, with total payments to Aramco reported to be close to $5 billion.

Transfer of ownership changed Aramco's functions. But it continues to have an intimate part in the Saudi economy. It builds and runs projects of first importance. These include use of gas, formerly flared wastefully, to produce electric power for burgeoning industries. It also builds and operates power plants, refineries, and other technical enterprises. It pushes oil exploration, adding new proven reserves offsetting the huge exports. Aramco's four parent companies also take part in such activities. Thus, Saudi Arabia benefits from highly important technical and management skills, which it badly needs. Its nationals gain experience for the future.

From the beginning, Saudi Arabia's American partners actively helped to develop both material and human resources. Besides oil operations, they drilled water wells and pioneered agricultural projects. As already described (Chapter 4), they trained Saudis in many branches of work. Currently, Saudis hold about half of Aramco's management and supervisory positions. Saudis have sat on Aramco's board for some time.

By creating outstanding working relations with the government, Aramco is seen as an enlightened and helpful company, not as an exploiter. For its part, Aramco and its parent companies benefit from providing services and have had favorable access to oil for export.

The statistics of modernizing the economy are impressive. Gross domestic product (GDP), measured in constant prices, grew by 9.8 percent compounded in the years 1975–80 during the Second Development Plan. But significantly the oil sector grew only 5.0 percent while the nonoil sector grew by 15.7 percent. For a time there was rapid inflation. Under the development plans spending was pushed so rapidly that during the years 1971–77 the cost of living about tripled. The total money supply grew from 3.78 billion riyals in the latter part of 1972 to 45.30 billion riyals in mid-1978. Since then it has been in better control.[8]

The development plans naturally seek to rely as much as possible on the Saudis themselves. Thus, the plans expand education and training so that Saudis can take more responsibility in place of foreigners.

Underlying all is care to safeguard Islamic religious and moral values while taking advantage of modern technology. Education long centered upon religious and classical instruction at the mosques. But traditionally that was available only to males, to a few in the towns, and not to the nomads. In 1952 only 42,000 boys and no girls were in school. Illiteracy was said to be about 95 percent. Hardly any had been educated abroad.

The Third Development Plan allocated to education about a sixth of total outlay, providing for expansion at all levels. As of 1980–81 there were about 1.5 million students in 8,223 schools and 3,684 students in vocational training centers. For girls, education began only about 1960, influenced by the wife of then Prince Faysal ibn Abd al-Aziz. By 1980–81 about 37 percent of students were girls. In education the sexes are separated because of long-standing social, cultural, and religious convictions. Adult education was also being pushed, with 142,370 male and female students. There were also six universities comprising 54 colleges and institutes.[9] These institutions will have opportunity to carry forward the historic Arab and Islamic achievements in both pioneering and spreading knowledge in the fields of mathematics and other branches of science.[10]

As of 1981 there were 22 social service and community development centers, to give free aid to those in need. A social insurance system covering more than 1 million persons now provided regular income in case of retirement and disability, and to surviving dependents in case of death. As urbanization proceeded, municipalities were helped to provide water, sewage, and drainage facilities. The Third

Development Plan aimed at providing 267,000 new housing units, about two thirds by the private sector.[11] There were 66 hospitals, five of which had the latest medical equipment, and 889 health centers and dispensaries. These services were being expanded.[12] The many public facilities, along with funds readily available for personal needs (including cheap loans for housing and business requirements), have vastly improved the people's standard of living.

Beginning with the reign of King Abd al-Aziz the trend was for more and more Saudis to be trained outside the country. Prince Faysal ibn Abd al-Aziz was a leader in support of study abroad. Seven of his eight sons went to the United States to study, first in preparatory schools and then in colleges and universities. His son Prince Saud, a Princeton graduate, became foreign minister. This is the post in which Faysal himself served with such distinction before becoming king. Many top leaders, including as of 1979 ten of the twenty-six members of King al-Khalid's cabinet, studied at American institutions. The portfolios of these ten included, besides foreign affairs, petroleum, industry, agriculture and water, commerce, labor, and information. Governor al-Qurayshi of the Monetary Agency, who has a degree in business administration from the University of Southern California, is quoted as saying: "In my mind the lack of enough skilled manpower is still the number-one problem in this country. . . . We have Saudi Arabs who are highly qualified, but not yet in sufficient numbers. We need quantity as well as quality."[13] The trend in 1981, however, was to give more and more training at home, strengthening advanced educational institutions.

The development programs, with rapid expansion of construction, called for a labor force far larger than Saudi Arabia could supply. Continuing great expansion of the economy readily absorbed the labor of the cities and towns. And many of the nomadic tribesmen, never more than about a fourth of the total population, variously estimated at 4 million to 8 million excluding resident foreigners, were not accustomed to regular work. Aramco pioneered in employing and training these nomads, and the government has been offering them training. Also, it offers special inducements to shift to agriculture and to employment in business and industry.

Training efforts are highly important for the future. But developing an adequate pool of national workers is a task of many years. Meanwhile, the current development could not have taken place without the coming of large numbers of skilled artisans and unskilled laborers, along with many technicians. As of 1982 about 2 million foreigners were in the country. About half were Arabs from other countries, largely from Yemen, and most of the rest were Asian. Tens of thousands of Western and other technicians worked on projects. The presence of so many unassimilated foreigners raises problems, now and for the future.

No country of so large an area has ever been so rapidly and greatly changed—and so enriched—as has Saudi Arabia in the past generation. Oil has not been an unmixed blessing. No country could carry out a crash program of development, costing hundreds of billions, without waste, confusion, financial abuses, speculation, and new riches often recklessly squandered. More than 2,500 years ago the prophet Micah asked a question relevant to Saudi Arabia today, and gave good advice:

Ministry buildings in modern Riyadh (courtesy of Aramco)

Riyadh buildings under construction, 1980 (courtesy of Aramco World Magazine. Photographed by S. M. Amin)

Will the Lord be pleased with thousands of rams, or with ten thousands
of rivers of oil? . . . What doth the Lord require of thee, but to do justly,
and to have mercy, and to walk humbly with thy God. (Micah 6 : 6–8)

Acceptance of new ways of life by a people who until quite recently lived much as in Micah's time cannot be easy. Old and new
social, economic, and religious cultures clash. How can the new ways,
adopted so extensively by the government and a large number of the
Saudi people, be made acceptable to the many who are steeped in
old ways and traditions? What will be the long-run effects of sudden
increase of wealth, hothouse development, urbanization, wholesale
education, and experience with the vastly different outside world?
How far will the ambitious economic projects succeed? (The Saudis
are determined that these will not become, as some skeptics have
feared, the Saudi "pyramids.")

To speculate about these questions is beyond the scope of this work.
But experience elsewhere in today's world shows that modernizing
and stabilizing a poor and traditional society is a long, complicated,
and risky process. It cannot be accomplished in a single generation,
but Saudi Arabia's rulers have given impressive leadership in this
difficult task.

THE OPEC CONNECTION

OPEC's near-monopoly power has been a basic factor in boosting
Saudi Arabia's income. OPEC was founded in 1960 by Saudi Arabia,
Iran, Iraq, Kuwait, and Venezuela at a conference at Baghdad.[14]

OPEC's creation was part of the growing nationalism that has led
developing countries that export oil to gain greater control over its
production by foreigners. During the 1970s, and until the oil glut of
1981–82, OPEC's control of oil gave it enough monopoly power to
raise prices drastically. Also, it gave Saudi Arabia and the other Arab
members leverage in international affairs. In early May 1973, King
Faysal passed important messages to Washington via Aramco officials. He stressed the "deep-seated" Saudi-American friendship. But
he also emphasized that "Zionism and along with it the Commu-
nists" were jeopardizing American interests in the area. The tide of

Arab opinion "was now running so heavily against America" that he was "not able to stand alone much longer" among the Arab countries. At the same time, a Saudi official told the Aramco officials that Egypt might "embark on some sort of hostilities" against Israel. The thrust of these warnings, which were repeated in June, was the urge for an American initiative to press for a settlement of the Arab-Israeli struggle. Aramco representatives brought these warnings to the White House and the State Department. But the seriousness of the warnings was not recognized. Also, President Nixon was deeply involved in Watergate, and nothing was done.[15]

After the war of Egypt and Syria against Israel began in October the warning was urgently repeated through Aramco. When the United States nevertheless resupplied Israel, King Faysal announced the embargo against the United States and a number of other nations, in which other Arab states joined. And he cut back oil output by about one fourth.[16]

The use of monopoly power by OPEC's members, deriving from the vast oil deposits given them by the chance of nature, was a major event in history. It severely disrupted the world economy, which was based upon cheap energy; slowed its growth; and conferred vast wealth on these countries. From 1960 through 1973 OPEC's total revenues from oil grew tenfold, to $93 billion. (In that period demand for oil grew, and OPEC added eight members.) From 1974 through 1981 the total soared more than thirteenfold, to about $1,250 billion. Meanwhile, importers paid much more than that for imported oil. The yearly cost of United States oil imports grew nearly tenfold from 1973 to 1981, to about $76 billion (see Appendix I, Table 8). In 1980 total revenues from oil of OPEC members were $264 billion, more than the GDP of all but seven of the richest nations. Thus, eleven of OPEC's thirteen members, with little more than 2 percent of the world's people, were paid nearly nine tenths of these huge sums by non-OPEC countries. The remainder went to populous Indonesia and Nigeria, with about 5 percent of the world's population.[17]

The embargo of 1973 was followed by a scramble for oil by the importing countries. Prices varied widely and were sharply higher. When the embargo was lifted early in 1974, prices ranged from about three to four times higher than before the 1973 war. Prices continued rising, as OPEC tested the buyers of oil.

From early 1974 through 1978 price increases did not outrun American inflation. But much larger increases began in 1979. Iran's revolution, which began early in that year, drastically cut oil output, causing shortages and urgent buying at erratic and sharply higher prices, especially for spot delivery. That, coupled with later outbreak of the Iran-Iraq war, reduced the combined output of the two countries from 7.8 million bpd in 1978 to 2.2 million bpd in September 1981.[18] A further factor influencing Arab members of OPEC was the Egypt-Israel agreement of March 1979 at Camp David, to which they objected because Egypt had made peace without insisting on a solution of the Palestine problem. Average basic prices per barrel rose from $13.77 in January 1979 to $37.07 in 1981. That is more than nine times the average in 1973, before the embargo. In real terms, allowing for American inflation, the increase was more than four times as great.[19]

Saudi Arabia went along with the drastic price increases. But it argued in OPEC for stable prices and some degree of moderation. It has a stake in worldwide stability. Its leaders are aware of the risk of social and international dangers, as ever higher prices upset the world economy and add to inflation. To press fellow members to agree to a fixed basic price, Saudi Arabia kept production at around 9 to 10 million bpd from 1979 through most of 1981. That raised its share of OPEC production from around one third in 1977 to nearly half in September 1981.[20]

Finally, Shaykh Ahmad Zaki Yamani, the longtime Saudi minister of petroleum, won out. In the fall of 1981 OPEC members reluctantly agreed to a fixed price of $34 per barrel for basic Saudi crude, with differentials based on quality and location. A limit of 17.5 million bpd for OPEC production was set early in 1982. The fixed price, it was announced, was to hold through 1982. But events that followed shocked OPEC. Price increases had gone too far and too fast, in light of the changing conditions. A glut followed, and oil came to be offered for less than $34, often under $30.

After 1973 the sharp run-up of prices reduced the worldwide demand for oil. But, despite the enormous costs, it taught the world a lesson: to stop wasting a precious finite resource. It led to conservation and more efficient use in factories and houses. United States imports of petroleum and products fell from nearly 9 million bpd in 1977 to 6 million bpd in 1981. The huge American demand for gasoline shrank, as the average fuel efficiency of automobiles greatly increased. The drop of about 20 percent in oil production in non-Communist countries from 1979 to September 1981 indicated a like drop in consumption.[21] Also, the fall in demand for oil was aggravated by the acute worldwide recession. Furthermore, there was a shift to other energy sources such as coal, waterpower, and nuclear power. United States imports of oil fell to 4.68 million bpd in the first quarter of 1982 and after 1973 non-OPEC production grew.[22]

To support the price of $34 Saudi Arabia cut back production, first to 8.5 million bpd in the fall of 1981, and early in 1982 to 7 million bpd. By August 1982 well-informed sources indicated that Saudi production was down to 4.5 million bpd. But the glut continued, with major widespread effects. From 1979 to the spring of 1982 OPEC's total production fell by nearly half, from 30.9 million bpd to 16 million bpd. (Total OPEC capacity is about 35 million bpd.) And in that period OPEC's share of total non-Communist production fell from 63 percent to well under half.[23] The lower prices for oil forced many OPEC members to cut spending for development, and in some cases even to borrow.

The oil glut had further ramifications. Cheaper oil lessened the pressure for more economical use, both in industry and for personal needs. Many projects that relied upon ever higher oil prices were canceled or postponed. Such projects included worldwide exploration for oil, synthetic production from Colorado shale and Canadian oil sands, and the gas pipeline from Alaska through Canada to the United States. Also, cheaper gasoline led to increased use.

No one can safely predict the future of oil prices. The Middle East is unstable, with Iran and Iraq at war and Israeli-Arab tension. In the spring of 1982 there was sharp dissension among the members of OPEC, with a split between Islamic moderates and radicals. Some of the latter even made threats against Saudi Arabia and other moderate states. Apart from political differences, members were differing about policies of production and pricing. Saudi Arabia, superior in output, reserves, and financial strength, argued for stable prices and ending limits on production once the glut disappeared. Others wanted the maximum possible return for their lesser production, and to make the most sooner from their lesser reserves. They wanted OPEC to continue controls on production and to use its muscle for higher prices as soon as conditions permitted. Saudi Arabia was in a strong position, with 40 percent of OPEC's output in the spring of 1982, and capacity to raise output from the then current 6.5 million bpd to 10 million bpd or more.

Whatever the outcome it is clear that, with oil and finance occupying center stage, Saudi Arabia finds itself projected into the midst of world affairs.

ECONOMIC POWER AND INTERNATIONAL INVOLVEMENT

While Saudi Arabia, with its power in oil and finance, has become a major factor in the world economy, it has the misfortune to be strategically located in the midst of the chronic turmoil of the Middle East. Thus, it cannot remain aloof from the resulting problems.

Since the time of King Abd al-Aziz, Saudi Arabia has been forced more and more to have an active foreign policy. Unlike him, King Faysal had broad foreign experience and, like his father, was highly regarded in the Arab and Islamic world until his untimely assassination in 1975. His part in the oil embargo of 1973 is described in the previous section. His son, Foreign Minister Prince Saud al-Faysal, is able and active in foreign affairs.

The huge payments to OPEC for oil, after the dramatic run-up of prices in 1973–74, destabilized the world financial system. The current account surplus of OPEC members rose from $5 billion in 1973 to $74 billion the next year. Nevertheless, the system managed to "recycle" the huge payments with less trouble than was feared. OPEC members bought much more abroad, imports of Saudi Arabia alone totaling well over $100 billion from 1974 through 1981. Also, they paid big sums for foreign labor and services. Some, notably Saudi Arabia, invested large sums abroad. Foreign governments, banks, some OPEC members, OPEC, and international agencies made loans and grants to less developed countries (LDC's) needing help. By 1978, OPEC's current account surplus in the system of international payments had fallen to about $5 billion. But the huge increase of oil prices after 1978 was again destabilizing. That surplus rose to about $60 billion in 1979 and to a peak of about $110 billion in 1980. For 1981 it was estimated to be down to about the 1979 level and was falling rapidly as the oil glut cut into the revenues of OPEC members.[24]

The industrialized countries were able to cope, but at high cost. But the LDC's, especially those not producing oil, were hard hit. High oil costs have been wiping out much of such gains as the LDC's have been able to make in the face of rapid population growth. They have an interest in pressing OPEC and its members for moderation in pricing and for large continuing aid. Each developing country must cope as best it can by its own efforts. But that is not enough. External help is needed, and they have had to borrow heavily, largely because of the high cost of oil. The public and publicly guaranteed foreign debt of non-oil-developing countries grew from $75.9 billion at the end of 1973 to a projected $279.5 billion at the end of 1980. A further increase of about $40 billion in 1981 of the foreign debt of LDC's was indicated. Some of these had borrowed beyond the limits of prudence, and payments had to be stretched out and/or interest payments adjusted. Banks had loaned heavily and could not safely do much more. Collapse of a major borrower or bank could gravely affect the world's financial system.[25]

The industrial countries have helped individually. The World Bank made loans to nonoil LDC's to help them develop their own energy resources. The International Monetary Fund first set up a modest fund to aid LDC's with problems caused by high oil prices. In 1977 it proposed a $10 billion fund, which began operating in 1979. To this the United States, Canada, several European countries, and Japan contributed. Saudi Arabia and some other OPEC members also took part, recognizing their responsibility for, as well as their interest in, a stable world economy. Saudi Arabia contributed about $52 million to the first IMF fund. To the second and larger fund it made the largest pledge, about $2.5 billion compared with $1.9 billion by the United States. Up to May 1981 Saudi Arabia had loaned about $3 billion to the World Bank and about $6 billion to the IMF. It then agreed to make further loans to the latter, for its fund to help countries with serious payment problems, up to 4 billion SDR's in the first year, and up to a total of 8 billion SDR's over six years (the SDR equaled $1.18 in May 1981).[26]

The great amount of Saudi Arabia's aid is not generally realized. Besides contributing to the IMF funds, Saudi Arabia, in the period from 1976 to 1980, provided aid totaling $20 billion to sixty countries for economic and social development. About 40 percent of this was in the form of grants, and the rest "soft" loans of which about half was a grant element. Thus, Saudi aid was about 6 percent of the country's GDP; it was 41 percent of total OPEC aid, which totaled about $8 billion yearly as of 1981; and 15 percent of similar aid provided by industrial countries. (Aid by the United States is much less than 1 percent of GDP and is a smaller proportion of GDP than that of any industrialized country except Italy.) In providing part of this aid Saudi Arabia joined with other Arab and Islamic nations, subscribing more than 20 percent of the $15 billion total capital of twelve regional development institutions.[27]

Saudi Arabia and other OPEC countries, like developed countries, find that giving effective aid is far from easy. To provide cheaper oil would be discrimination, and it might only be resold at a profit. Grants are often squandered by waste and/or corruption. Developing countries are commonly mismanaged with unsound policies and are ravaged by acute inflation; all are short of trained personnel.

Saudi Arabia worries, and with reason, about threats to its internal and external security. Control of its oil and financial assets is a tempting prize. It cannot disregard the threat of subversion, attempted by unfriendly radical Islamic states or their agents or by dissidents. The seizure of Mecca's Grand Mosque in 1979 and riots by Shiites in Qatif a few months later were warnings that have been heeded. Iran, seeking to spread its fanatical Shiite revolution, showed surprising strength in the war with Iraq. It loomed as a worrisome danger to Saudi Arabia and the other moderate Gulf states. Along with Libya's Qaddafi, it made threats against them. Let us hope that Iran comes to its senses and sees that its greatest danger is from bordering Soviet Russia. Saudi Arabia also has cause to worry about Russia, with its foothold in South Yemen and over the horizon in Afghanistan and Ethiopia. Britain no longer polices the Persian-Arabian Gulf, and the United States is far away.

It has been risky for an Arab or Islamic country to appear to be too close to the United States, because of American favoritism to Israel. Their view of Israel as their number one enemy was reinforced in mid-1982, by Israel's bloody and destructive invasion of Lebanon. They blamed the United States for arming and then not restraining Israel—and for not making a major effort over the years toward solving the problem of the Palestinian people, deprived of their homeland.

The Arab-Israeli situation has long affected Saudi-American relations, notably at the time of the oil embargo of 1973. Thus, in 1979 it was not realistic for the United States to urge Saudi Arabia to support the Camp David agreements, whereby Egypt made peace without a settlement of the Palestinian situation. When those agreements were made, as Oxford's Professor Mabro put it, the Saudis "were given two choices: the fire or the frying pan": either oppose that settlement at the risk of "jeopardizing their special relationship with the United States, [and] of destabilizing Sadat's Egypt" or "accept Camp David at the risk of betraying their Arab responsibilities and the national feelings of their own population, thus putting their own internal security at risk."[28] Refusing to face such danger the Saudis had to choose the former risk, which fortunately did not materialize.

Saudi Arabia was again brought sharply to the fore in the United States in 1981 by the hard-fought issue of sale of AWACS (airborne warning and control systems planes) and other advanced arms. Many Americans then argued that Saudi Arabia—and Egypt too—should grant American bases in return for aid. But again that was not realistic. To do this would open the Saudi government to the charge by present or future opponents of being "stooges" of the United States. Furthermore, such action would put Soviet Russia in position to justify seeking more bases nearby.

The peace plan that the then heir apparent, Prince Fahd, put forward in 1981 was imaginative and constructive. It had been discussed with moderate Arab states, and also with the Palestine Liberation

Organization (PLO). It stated Saudi hopes for a just peace. Israel strongly objected, but the plan was generally supported by moderate Arab states, by the nations of Western Europe, and in many respects by the United States. Israeli withdrawal from occupied Arab lands would accord with UN Resolution 242, which both the United States and the Soviet Union approved. Insistence on restoring the holy places in East Jerusalem to Arab control has long been an emotional issue for the Saudis. Muslims believe that the Prophet Muhammad ascended to heaven from Jerusalem, and to them it is the holiest city after Mecca and Medina. It is also a most sacred place to Jews and Christians. The United States and most other countries refuse to recognize Jerusalem as Israel's capital, keeping their embassies at Tel Aviv. The plan also would confirm the right of the Palestinian people to return to the West Bank and the Gaza Strip, with a transitional period under UN supervision. There would be a Palestinian state with Jerusalem as its capital. States in the region would have the right to live in peace, with guarantees by the UN or some of its members. That was taken to mean accepting Israel's right to exist. But the radical Arab states summarily rejected the plan.

Saudi Arabia has maintained at least formal relations with these states and has given support to the PLO. Saudi Arabia is not militarily strong compared with such neighbors as Egypt, Syria, Iraq, and Iran, not to mention Israel, and seeks to contain conflicts in the Arab world and the Middle East.

By approving sale of AWACS the United States recognized that Saudi Arabia's central strategic position, its oil, and its constructive influence in the Arab and Islamic world make it important for Western interests and security. But the narrow margin of congressional approval was less than reassuring to the Saudis. As far back as 1947 Abd al-Aziz, in talking with Minister Childs, raised a question that is still revelant. The king wondered "how far and in what manner he might rely upon the United States."[29] His successors still wonder.

Saudi Arabia, along with other moderate Arab states, has wanted from the United States long-term support of territorial integrity and security.[30] Israel's adventure of mid-1982 in Lebanon, with apparent American acquiescence, greatly changed the Middle East situation. The humiliation of Arab countries by Israel took advantage of their disunity, and of the Iran-Iraq war. The oil glut made impracticable a protest such as the oil embargo of 1973. Also Egypt, the strongest Arab country, was neutralized by the Camp David peace with Israel. Meanwhile, there had been no significant progress, under the other chief part of the Camp David agreements, toward solving the thorny problem of the homeless Palestinian people, as to which UN Resolution 242 was a guide.

The events of mid-1982 opened the way for constructive initiatives in the Middle East. But they risked promoting radicalism in Arab and Islamic countries, created difficulties for those that were pro-American, and enlarged opportunities for the Soviet Union to advance its interests in the Middle East. Also, the heads of the European Common Market countries, which were already troubled by aspects of American foreign policy, issued a "vigorous condemnation" of the Israeli invasion. They called for "satisfying the legitimate aspirations of the Palestinian people." Belgian Prime Minister Wilfried Martens said that the United States was "cruelly isolated" with Israel.[31] How the events of June 1982 would affect Saudi Arabia, its special relationship with the United States, and its relations to other countries remained to be seen.

Saudi Arabia's system of rule by the king and royal family, with growing responsibility of other leaders, is unique. A cabinet with many highly trained men advises the king, with a few senior princes having final authority. Many princes work in other branches of government, some as provincial governors, and in the armed forces. Many outside the royal family have become influential, such as Petroleum Minister Yamani, Finance Minister Aba al-Khayl, and Governor al-Qurayshi of the Saudi Arabia Monetary Agency. The aim is a consensus of the royal family; other emerging leaders in the government and the economy; the *ulema,* or religious leaders; and prominent members of the tribes. Ties with the tribes have developed as a result of Abd al-Aziz's marriages with daughters of tribal leaders. Also, modern transport and communications, along with dispensing funds for individual benefits and local improvements, help to hold the country together.

In view of the historical trend away from royal rule, the leaders have felt the need for change. They have talked of broadening the government by setting up a consultative body, establishing local councils in cities and towns, and having a document about government functioning that would be a sort of constitution. But action has not yet materialized. Also, there have been steps to tighten spending and to curb big commissions and corruption.

Especially while the AWACS issue was pending, questions were raised about stability of the Saudi government. In the troubled Middle East great uncertainty about the course of events at home and abroad faces Saudi Arabia, along with many other countries. But the Saudi system has worked surprisingly well, considering the unavoidable difficulties of change from an undeveloped desert land to a rich and powerful nation. The House of Saud is able and backed by a tradition of generations of rule. When King Khalid died in June 1982, the transition to King Fahd's leadership was smooth. The Islamic religion is a central force. Conditions are far different from those in Iran, and Shiite Muslims are a tiny minority. The system of the *majlis,* under which all citizens can take complaints in person to the leaders of the central government and provincial governors, is a source of strength. Prosperity is widespread. Free education, medical and welfare services, and cheap homeownership are readily available to all Saudi citizens. No strong internal opposition is apparent, although the seizure of the Grand Mosque in Mecca by religious fanatics in 1979,[32] and Sadat's assassination in 1981, made clear the danger from radical elements, within or without.

Saudi Arabia's rulers and people have the awesome problem of how best to meld an age-old traditional society, with its historic religion and culture, into what the Covenant of the League of Nations called "the strenuous conditions of the modern world." And this has to be done in a time made historically brief by the rapid development of great economic and financial strength. The effects of imported Western ideas, widespread education, and the furious pace of economic growth are yet to be fully felt.

Saudi Arabia has made outstanding progress in operating the national finances. There is progress also in administration and management. But in the long run to operate the modern-type economy calls for developing a national force of workers—technical, skilled, and unskilled—to avoid relying so greatly on foreigners. And there remains the hard problem of finding ways to use adequately the abilities of the half of the country's people who are women. Dealing with the array of basic problems is a matter of decades.

Saudi Arabia has come a long way during the past half century. Its rulers and people have so far managed quite well the transition from a fledgling desert state to a nation with a key position in the Middle East and in world affairs. Let us wish them well.

APPENDIXES

I. TABLES

TABLE I
Oil Revenue, 1938–81
(millions of dollars)

Year	Amount	Year	Amount	Year	Amount
1938	0.1	1951	110.0	1966	789.7
1939	3.2	1952	212.2	1967	909.1
1940	1.2	1953	169.8	1968	926.8
1941	1.0	1954	236.3	1969	949.0
1942	1.1	1955	340.8	1970	1,214.0
1943	1.1	1956	290.2	1971	1,884.9
1944	1.7	1957	296.3	1972	2,744.6
1945	4.3	1958	297.6	1973	4,340.0
1946	10.4	1959	313.1	1974	22,573.5
1947	18.0	1960	333.7	1975	25,676.2
1948	52.5[a]	1961	377.6	1976	30,754.9
1949	39.1	1962	409.7	1977	36,540.1
1950	56.7	1963	607.7[b]	1978	32,233.8
		1964	523.2	1979	48,435.1
		1965	662.6	1980	84,466.4
				1981	101,200.0

Source: Figures for 1938, 1940–45, and 1947–49 are from OPEC's *Annual Statistical Bulletin*, since I have found no Saudi Arabian source for those years. The other figures are from SAMA annual reports, except for 1981, which is from a SAMA statement reported in the *Wall Street Journal*, April 6, 1982, p. 31.

Note: Budget estimates since 1974 show oil revenue as about 90 percent of total revenue. Aramco currently pays about 97 percent of the oil revenue. Payments by other companies began in 1954 in relatively small amounts, as shown in the Saudi Arabian Monetary Agency's 1981 annual report, p. 139.

For the years before 1945 data provided by Aramco in 1951 show payments larger than those shown above, apparently including advances, as follows (millions of dollars):

1938	0.34	1941	3.45
1939	3.21	1942	3.41
1940	4.79	1943	1.32
		1944	1.66

[a] The 1948 figure looks like a clerical error. If revenue were proportionate to oil production (Table 3), it would be about $32 million instead of $52.5 million.

[b] Including for 1963 $152.5 million of payments by Aramco, which appear to be advances.

TABLE 2
Revenues, 1938–44
(millions of dollar equivalent)

Year	Pilgrimage	Customs	Other Local	Total Except Oil	Oil	Total
1938	2.63	3.67	.53	6.83	.34	7.17
1939	1.31	2.31	.56	4.18	3.21	7.39
1940	1.31	2.31	.62	4.24	4.79	9.03
1941	—	—	—	2.20	3.45	5.65
1942	—	—	—	1.90	3.41	5.31
1943	—	1.80	2.39	4.19	1.32	5.51
1944	3.00	1.50	3.00	7.50	1.66	9.16

SOURCE: Data, partly estimated, from Aramco, 1951. Figures for 1945, the last war year, are not available. Receipts in 1940–43 include advances by the oil company (Table 1).

TABLE 3
Oil Production, 1938–81
(millions of barrels)

Year	Aramco	Getty Oil	Arabian Oil	Total	Average per Day
1938	0.5	—	—	0.5	
1939	3.9	—	—	3.9	
1940	5.1	—	—	5.1	
1941	4.3	—	—	4.3	
1942	4.5	—	—	4.5	
1943	4.9	—	—	4.9	
1944	7.8	—	—	7.8	
1945	21.3	—	—	21.3	
1946	59.9	—	—	59.9	
1947	89.9	—	—	89.9	
1948	142.9	—	—	142.9	
1949	174.0	—	—	174.0	
1950	199.5	—	—	199.5	
1951	278.0	—	—	278.0	
1952	301.9	—	—	301.9	
1953	308.3	—	—	308.3	
1954	347.8	3.0	—	350.8	
1955	352.2	4.4	—	356.6	

Year	Aramco	Getty Oil	Arabian Oil	Total	Average per Day
1956	360.9	5.8	—	366.8	
1957	362.1	11.6	—	373.7	
1958	370.5	14.7	—	385.2	
1959	399.8	21.2	—	421.0	
1960	456.4	24.9	—	481.4	
1961	508.3	28.7	3.7	540.5	
1962	555.1	33.7	11.0	599.8	
1963	594.6	33.1	24.0	651.7	
1964	628.1	34.4	31.6	694.1	
1965	739.1	33.0	32.8	804.9	2.20
1966	873.3	30.2	46.1	949.7	2.60
1967	948.1	25.1	50.6	1,023.8	2.80
1968	1,035.8	23.2	54.7	1,113.7	3.04
1969	1,092.3	22.7	58.8	1,173.9	3.21
1970	1,295.3	28.7	6.26	1,386.7	3.79
1971	1,641.6	33.7	65.3	1,740.6	4.76
1972	2,098.4	28.5	75.0	2,202.0	6.01
1973	2,677.1	23.5	71.9	2,772.6	7.59
1974	2,996.5	29.8	68.7	3,095.1	8.47
1975	2,491.8	31.2	59.5	2,582.5	7.07
1976	3,053.9	29.7	55.7	3,139.3	8.57
1977	3,291.2	32.0	34.8	3,358.0	9.20
1978	2,952.3	29.4	56.3	3,038.0	8.32
1979	3,376.4	30.2	72.6	3,479.2	9.53
1980	3,525.3	28.5	70.0	3,623.8	9.90
1981	3,513.2	27.2	45.6	3,586.0	9.82

SOURCE: SAMA annual reports, 1960–61, p. 49; 1975, p. 110; 1981, p. 138.

TABLE 4

British Sovereign Rates in Riyals and Dollars at Jidda, 1945–52

	British Sovereign, George Head (in riyals)		British Sovereign, George Head (in dollars)	
	High	Low	High	Low
1945 (8/15–12/31)	71.25	57.50	21.00	18.50
1946	89.00	60.00	20.00	17.50
1947	69.00	58.00	16.50	14.00
1948	68.00	52.25	16.00	12.75
1949	62.25	45.00	13.25	11.65
1950	58.75	41.00	12.00	10.25
1951	49.32	42.25	13.00	11.70
1952	45.14	40.07	12.23	10.80

SOURCES: Most data are from records of Netherlands Trading Society and Banque de l'Indochine (quotations to April 1947 are from Aramco). For monthly rates see *Middle East Journal*, vol. 7, nos. 3 and 4 (1953), pp. 364–66.

TABLE 5

Coins and Coinage

Coins

Gold	Weight (grams)	Fineness	Weight of Fine Metal (grams)
British sovereign	7.98805	.916$\frac{2}{3}$	7.32238*
Saudi Arabian sovereign	7.98805	.91666	7.32232
Silver			
Riyal	11.6638	.916$\frac{2}{3}$	10.6918**
$\frac{1}{2}$ Riyal	5.8319	.916$\frac{2}{3}$	5.3459
$\frac{1}{4}$ Riyal	2.916	.916$\frac{2}{3}$	2.673
Minor			
Qirsh	6.5 ⎫		⎧ 22 qirsh
$\frac{1}{2}$ Qirsh	5.5 ⎬	75% copper	⎨ equal to
$\frac{1}{4}$ Qirsh	4.25 ⎭	25% nickel	⎩ 1 riyal

*This is the equivalent of 113.0016 grains, or .23542 oz.
**This is the equivalent of 165 grains, or .34375 oz.

Coinage
I. Silver Riyals

Period	Amount Coined	Cumulative Total
1936–39	7,200,000	7,200,000
1940–45	63,000,000	70,200,000
1946–48	28,300,000	98,500,000
1949	60,000,000	158,500,000
1950	nil	158,500,000
1951	50,000,000	208,500,000
1952	77,000,000	285,500,000

II. Minor Coins
The following cupronickel coins were obtained in 1947:

	Number	Value in Riyals
1 qirsh	7,150,000	325,000
½ qirsh	10,850,000	246,591
¼ qirsh	21,500,000	244,318
Total		815,909

III. Gold Sovereigns

	Ordered	Arrived in Saudi Arabia
1951	1,000,000	100,000
1952	1,000,000	1,200,000
1953 (to May 1)	nil	200,000
Total	2,000,000	1,500,000

Also in 1945 and 1947 91,210 and 121,364 gold discs, respectively, were coined, and during 1953 a million more sovereigns.

IV. Place of Minting
In 1941–43, 15 million riyals were coined in Bombay; in 1944–49, 72 million in the United States; in 1949, 20 million in England; and in 1949–52, 157 million in Mexico. The gold discs were coined in the United States, and the gold sovereigns in France.

SOURCE: United States Mint annual reports; FRUS 1941 III, p. 639, and 1943 IV, p. 858; and the writer's records.

TABLE 6
Budget for Fiscal Year 1370–71
(ending March 16, 1953)

Revenues

	Percent of Budget	Riyals	Dollar Equivalent (approx.)
			(millions)
Taxes, mostly on income (mostly Aramco)	48.7%	SR 356.0	$ 96.4
Royalties	30.1	220.8	59.7
Foreign trade revenue	10.3	75.2	20.3
Pilgrims and travelers	2.3	16.8	4.5
Government enterprises	3.0	22.3	6.0
Other	1.5	10.9	2.9
Issue of new coins	4.1	30.0	8.1
Total	100.0%	SR 732.0	$197.9

Expenditures

	Percent of Budget	Riyals	Dollar Equivalent (approx.)
General development, including agriculture	21.5%	SR 163.1	$ 44.0
Defense, including installations	17.8	135.2	36.5
"Riyadh affairs"	13.6	103.1	27.9
Internal security and subsidy to tribes	10.4	79.1	21.4
Ministries, departments, etc.	9.9	75.0	20.3
Health, education, social and religious services	5.3	39.8	10.7
Government enterprises	3.3	25.2	6.8
Debts	13.2	100.0	27.0
Purchase of new coins	4.0	30.0	8.1
Reserves and adjustments	1.0	7.5	2.0
Total	100.0%	SR 758.0	$204.7

SOURCE: Translation of the budget provided by the Saudi Arabian government.

TABLE 7

World Crude Oil Production, Excluding Natural Gas Liquids, 1977–81
(million barrels per day)

	1977	1978	1979	1980	1981 [p] (September)	1981 [p]
World	59.7	60.2	62.7	59.5	53.6	55.7
Non-Communist countries	46.7	46.4	48.6	45.2	39.4	41.5
OPEC	26.8	29.8	30.9	26.9	20.4	22.7
Saudi Arabia	9.0	8.1	9.2	9.6	9.0	9.6
United States	8.2	8.7	8.6	8.6	8.6	8.6
Communist countries	13.0	13.8	14.0	14.2	14.2	14.2
USSR	10.7	11.2	11.5	11.7	11.8	11.8

OPEC Production, 1979–81
(million barrels per day)

	1979	1980	1981 September	1981 [p]
Saudi Arabia	9.3	9.6	9.0	9.6
Iraq	3.5	2.5	1.0	1.0
Iran	3.2	1.7	1.0	1.4
Venezuela	2.4	2.2	2.1	2.1
Nigeria	2.3	2.1	1.1	1.5
Kuwait	2.2	1.4	0.7	0.9
Libya	2.1	1.8	0.7	1.1
United Arab Emirates	1.8	1.7	1.5	1.5
Indonesia	1.6	1.6	1.6	1.6
Algeria	1.2	1.0	0.6	0.8
Neutral Zone (Saudi Arabia-Kuwait)	0.6	0.5	0.3	0.4
Qatar	0.5	0.5	0.4	0.4
Gabon	0.2	0.2	0.2	0.2
Ecuador	0.2	0.2	0.2	0.2
Totals	30.9	26.9	20.4	22.7

SOURCE: National Foreign Assessment Center, Central Intelligence Agency, Washington, D.C., *International Energy Statistical Review,* December 22, 1981, p. 1; April 27, 1982, p. 1. Figures for Saudi Arabia differ from Saudi official figures in Table 3.

[p] Preliminary.

TABLE 8

United States Imports of Petroleum and Products, 1979–81

	Quantity From (millions of barrels per day)			Price	Value
	Saudi Arabia	All Arab OPEC Members	All Countries	(dollars per barrel)[2]	(billions of dollars)[3]
1973	0.49	0.92	6.26	4.08	7.74
1974	0.46	0.75	6.11	12.52	26.26
1975	0.72	1.38	6.06	13.93	25.06
1976	1.23	2.42	7.31	13.48	32.11
1977	1.38	3.19	8.81	14.53	42.01
1978	1.14	2.96	8.36	14.57	39.60
1979	1.36	3.06	8.46	21.67	56.51
1980	1.28	2.55	6.91	33.89	74.44
1981	1.12	1.85	5.98	37.14	76.22[5]
1982[4]	—		4.68	—	—

SOURCE: National Energy Information Center, U.S. Department of Energy, Washington, D.C.: *Annual Report to Congress,* vol. 2 (1981), Tables 11, 22, 25, and 41; *Monthly Energy Review* (May 1981), pp. 31, 80.

1. Includes imports for the Strategic Petroleum Reserve, which began in 1977.
2. Refiner acquisition price of imported crude oil. The price in 1973 is estimated.
3. Includes refined petroleum products.
4. First quarter.
5. Preliminary.

TABLE 9

Expenditures and Estimates, August 21, 1971–April 23, 1982
(approximate equivalents in billions of dollars)*

	Projects, Estimates			Total Expenditures	
Fiscal Year Ended	Budgeted	Expected Shortfall	Amount Less Expected Shortfall	Budgeted	Actual
8/21/71	0.6			1.5	1.4
8/12/72	1.2			2.6	2.0
7/29/73	1.8			3.6	2.7
7/19/74	4.0			6.5	5.3
7/9/75	7.5			12.9	9.9
6/28/76	21.1			31.4	24.1
6/16/77	21.1	5.8	15.3	35.4	36.3
6/5/78	21.7	6.6	15.1	32.3	40.0
5/26/79	24.8	5.6	19.2	38.8	44.0
5/14/80	31.6	6.1	25.5	64.5	56.2
5/4/81	52.1			73.1	70.6[p]
4/23/82	60.0			89.0	—

SOURCE: SAMA annual reports, passim.

*Converted at 4.15 riyals per dollar for fiscal years 1971 and 1972; 3.70 for 1973; 3.53 for 1974–77; 3.45 for 1978; 3.35 for 1979–81; and 3.41 for 1982.

[p] Provisional estimate.

II. REPORT ON ESTABLISHMENT OF THE SAUDI ARABIAN MONETARY AGENCY*
Jidda, Saudi Arabia, February 1952

The desire of the Saudi Arabian Government to create a new institution to handle monetary affairs, to act as its fiscal agent and for financial and economic research shows an appreciation of the important part that such an institution can play in the country's progress. Most countries today have such institutions of one kind or another. They provide machinery that is necessary for the operation of a stable and convenient monetary system. They afford means to regulate local monetary and banking practices as may be appropriate. They make easier the handling of public receipts and payments and holding and transfer of funds. They give close and regular contact with foreign financial centers. They collect and analyze data about local and foreign financial conditions and thus are in position to advise the Government on important problems of policy.

I strongly recommend creation of the "Saudi Arabian Monetary Agency." Such an institution can, with careful and understanding management, promote the ends outlined above. Saudi Arabia has been growing so rapidly in resources that its existing financial machinery is inadequate or undeveloped in some important respects. The purpose of this report, which is based upon my preliminary report of November, 1951, and subsequent discussions, is to describe the kind of institution that in my opinion is best adapted to promoting the financial progress of Saudi Arabia.

Name and Location. A good name would be: "Saudi Arabian Monetary Agency." The operating headquarters should be at Jidda because this is the country's chief financial center. There should be offices or agencies in other important places as may be found appropriate.

*This report is substantially the same as the preliminary report submitted to Finance Minister Shaykh Abd Allah Sulayman in November 1951, with revision to take account of changes, mainly as to the institution's name and assuring regard for Islamic law, resulting from discussions with King Abd al-Aziz, Prince Saud, the minister, and others. The text herewith was included in an official publication in Arabic and English: "Saudi Arabian Government: Saudi Arabian Monetary Agency" (Al-Fateh National Press, Jidda, September 1952). This document, long out of print, contained the text of the royal decrees creating the agency, approving its charter and bylaws, and appointing George Blowers as governor.

Operations. The main operations should relate to: (1) currency affairs: (2) fiscal agency functions; and (3) financial and economic research.

(1) Currency functions. These would be:

(a) To stabilize and maintain the external and internal value of the currency.

(b) To hold and operate any monetary reserve funds as separate funds earmarked for monetary purposes only.

(c) To buy and sell for Government account gold and silver coin and bullion.

(d) To advise the Government about new coinage and handle the manufacture, shipment and issue of all coins, it being understood that coins would be issued only through and at the request of the Agency.

(e) To regulate commercial banks, exchange dealers and money changers as may be found appropriate.

There is now no adequate machinery to handle monetary affairs, e.g., to introduce the new gold sovereign and regulate its value, or to stabilize the value of silver and minor coins. There is no machinery for such regulation of foreign exchange dealing, banking or money changing as may be found appropriate. Whatever monetary measures the Government may eventually adopt, it needs new machinery.

The Agency should hold Saudi Arabia's currency reserve funds. These reserves should be treated as trust funds and set aside for monetary purposes only so that they cannot be diverted for ordinary expenditures. The size of such reserves and the nature of their use and control will depend upon the kind of action taken for monetary improvement.

(2) Fiscal agency functions. The receipts of all branches of the Government should be deposited in the Agency. Similarly all the Government's payments would be made from accounts in the Agency. The Agency thus would hold the Government's operating funds as well as its fiscal reserves. It would aid in controlling payments so that all branches of the Government would abide by the budget. The fiscal agency functions would be:

(a) To receive and act as depository for all the Government's foreign exchange revenues and fiscal reserves in accounts maintained abroad;

to be the Government's agent in making all payments for Government account in foreign exchange; and to sell foreign exchange for local and other currency, ordinarily only to banks and not to the public.

(b) To receive and act as depository for the revenues in local currency of all branches of the Government; to be the Government's agent to pay sums due in accordance with the authorized budget; and for these purposes to maintain such operating accounts as the Government through the Minister of Finance may direct.

Organization in the field of public finance has not kept pace with the rapid growth of revenues and expenditures that is due to expanding oil revenues. This growth has come so recently—in the past three years—that there has not been time to develop adequate machinery to handle receipts and payments. An organization that sufficed for the more simple society of Saudi Arabia of a dozen years ago and a yearly budget of SR25 million (say $7 million), cannot properly handle a budget more than twenty-five times as great.

In particular foreign exchange has become a major problem. At least four-fifths of the revenue now is in foreign currency, mainly from oil. Wise handling of foreign exchange transactions as well as wise use of the funds is vital to the country's stability and progress. The savings to the Government from careful centralized handling of foreign exchange would be very substantial and would justify creating the Agency apart from anything else.

The Agency could help the Government to use to best advantage the sterling and other non-dollar currencies received. Receipts of these currencies from all sources in 1951 may be estimated to be equivalent at free market rates to perhaps $30 million or about a fifth of total revenues in foreign exchange. Total purchases from the sterling countries in 1949 were of somewhat similar amount—later figures are not available. Hence in effect the Government can be viewed as a supplier of Saudi Arabia's needs for these currencies. The Agency could sell these currencies in an orderly way to the banks to meet the needs of importers and receive local currency in payment.

In order that the Agency acting as fiscal agent should not unduly curtail the activities which locally established banks and money changers may reasonably expect to continue, especially as to foreign exchange, it ordinarily should deal only with banks and not with the general public. On the one hand that would leave to the banks a normal and reasonable function. On the other hand it would avoid tying up the Agency's resources in non-governmental dealings. The Agency may ask Kaaki to act as its agent in some places where it may not be advisable to establish branches, and thus make use of his experience and organization.

The Government, besides having most of its receipts in foreign currency, has large payments to make in foreign currency. There should be a foreign currency budget included in the regular budget covering payments in foreign currency, and these payments should be made, subject to suitable control, directly from receipts. The nominal equivalent in local currency could be included in the general budget. Such foreign currency as is sold for local expenses could be sold by the Agency in an orderly way so as not to disturb the market.

The Government should build up local currency deposits in the Agency, as well as deposits abroad in foreign currency, on which it can draw for current expenses. This is better than relying as heretofore upon the lines of credit granted by local banks and the anticipation of future payments. Also it is important that the current receipts of all branches of the Government be deposited in the Agency and thus passed through the Ministry of Finance instead of being used directly by some receiving organizations.

The Agency could be of great value as agent for the Government in paying the budget and the Government's contractual obligations as per standing instructions to be given it. Of course it would have to be in possession of sufficient funds. If a system of receipt of revenues and punctual payment with priority of basic costs of Government and of definitive contractual obligations can be created through the Agency, the Government's credit and the efficiency of its operations would notably improve. This procedure also would simplify administrative procedures and save much work to the Ministry of Finance, and in particular to the Minister and the highest officials of the Ministry.

The experience of Venezuela is significant as to handling its large revenue from oil. Venezuela has a total population similar to Saudi Arabia, but only one-third of the area. Its reserves of oil are similarly large. Its current production was about 500,000 barrels daily in 1940, and has risen to about 1,700,000 daily at present. In 1940 Venezuela's Central Bank held total reserves of $31 million, but these have now risen to $373 million. Meanwhile Venezuela has made great progress from use of oil revenues for economic development, education and public health.

Saudi Arabia would do well to emulate Venezuela's example in building up gradually large financial reserves. These are needed to strengthen the currency. Also they are needed for fiscal purposes. Dependence upon a single item, oil, is so extreme that any material fall in the revenue from oil would be a shock to the country. The oil business in 1951–52 is booming. But it is subject to ups and downs, and the boom will not last forever. Saudi Arabia will act wisely if it builds a reserve to cushion any shock. The Agency could be invaluable to the Government in holding and administering such a reserve, and helping to determine where and in what form it should be held.

(3) Financial and economic research. This is of basic importance for the future and clearly would warrant setting up a special department in the Agency. The functions would be:

To collect and analyze financial and economic data in order to aid the Government and the Agency in formulating and carrying out financial and economic policies.

No machinery for economic research now exists in the Government. Financial and economic statistics are inadequate or do not exist. Permanent machinery for gathering and analyzing data is necessary to help the Government in formulating and carrying out wise financial and economic policies. The Official Gazette of September 7, 1951, contains a decision of the Ministry of Finance to establish a new office "to handle economic affairs." The Agency's department of economic research should work closely with the new economic office of the Ministry.

The Agency and Economic Development. Encouragement of economic development is of utmost importance to Saudi Arabia. Though the country's natural resources except for oil and some other minerals are definitely limited, they can be developed to an important extent and their utilization improved, notably through careful development and handling of water supply.

Procedure for handling development varies in different countries.

In some it is under a special board or commission which may include leading officials. In others a special institution has been created to promote development. Also development has been handled in some countries as a special department of a Government bank. The type of procedure which seems best adapted to Saudi Arabia is an important matter for separate determination.

The first problem is the source of funds for development. The Government's income is so excellent that revenues permit sizeable allocations, as in the budget for the current fiscal year. But besides funds spent directly through usual budgetary procedure, the Agency could act as agent for the Government if desired in administering advances of Government funds for local development projects. An example would be to finance local water development, which might bring to local farmers such extensive benefits that they could gradually repay part or all of the original cost of the improvements. Where local land values are enhanced by such development the local farmers might, for example, organize a cooperative association to take responsibility for repayment in whole or in part.

The procedure for carrying out a development program will call for consideration in detail. But the Agency even though not itself providing the funds would be in position as the Government's fiscal agent to help in carrying out such plans.

Operations Not to Be Undertaken. The Agency would be an important new departure for Saudi Arabia. Over a period of time it may be expected to grow and develop new activities under changing conditions as similar institutions in other countries have done. For the present, however, it will be wise to begin gradually with the essential functions, and to gain experience and confidence; and it will not be necessary or expedient to undertake certain activities which similar institutions elsewhere undertake.

Clearly the Agency should not act in any way conflicting with the teachings of the Islamic law, such as by paying or receiving interest.

Summarizing, the Agency should not undertake any of the following functions:

(a) Paying or receiving interest.
(b) Receiving private deposits.

(c) Making advances to the Government or to private parties.
(d) Engaging in trade or having an interest in any commercial, industrial or agricultural enterprise.
(c) Buying or holding fixed property except what the Agency reasonably needs for its operations.
(f) Issuing currency notes.

In other countries it is the general practice of similar institutions to deal with the public only to the extent necessary to carry out the country's basic monetary policy. Such institutions do not generally accept deposits from the general public or make loans to private parties. The existing commercial banks are in position to supply adequate facilities to the public.

The Agency's success will require all possible cooperation from the commercial banks. This is a further reason why it should not compete with them in receiving deposits or making loans. Similarly the Agency in buying and selling foreign exchange should ordinarily deal only with banks, and leave to these the dealings with private parties whose credit standing and needs they can most readily appraise. The Agency can and should gain the confidence of the commercial banks and often will be able to help them with their problems.

All of the Agency's capital would come from the Government as per the proposal made below. The Agency would not create credit by issue of currency notes or receive other than Government deposits. Hence it would not have loanable funds apart from the proceeds of public revenues, and these will be needed for the Government's use. In other countries loans to government have been the bane of many similar institutions. If the Agency were in position to make such loans they might soon tie up any free funds. Similarly the Agency should not make loans to private parties.

Also it is clear that the Agency should not engage in trade. It should keep its capital liquid and not tie it up in investments in any commercial, industrial or agricultural enterprise, or by holding fixed property beyond what it reasonably needs for its operations.

Saudi Arabia has long been used to metallic money, and under existing conditions it will be wise to continue a "hard money" system. The Agency, therefore, should not issue currency notes. But this does not mean that Saudi Arabia must forego the advantages of a convenient means of payment in larger denominations or of elasticity of the supply of money. These advantages can be gained to a material extent in other ways. Gold coins have a large value in proportion to size and weight. At present various foreign notes circulate to some extent in different parts of the country, especially Egyptian in the west and Indian and American in the east. At the time of the pilgrimage foreign notes are much in evidence to give needed elasticity to the currency. While less convenient than money directly interchangeable with national currency, use of these foreign notes can and does obviate carrying large amounts of specie. Also the commercial banks can be encouraged to facilitate transfers of money by development of the system of checking accounts. They can make wider use of cashiers' checks.

The Agency should be a service institution, not operating to seek a profit. It should aim to promote better operation of the country's monetary system and better administration of the national finances.

Capital. In view of the Agency's position as a public service institution, the Government should provide the entire capital. To give the Agency proper standing in Saudi Arabia and abroad and to give elasticity to its operations, the greater part of the capital should be in liquid funds over and above the initial outlay for buildings and equipment. Since the Agency would not make loans or receive public deposits it would not need capital to protect the public as creditors.

I recommend that the Agency have an authorized capital equivalent to 500,000 sovereigns (calculated at $12 and equivalent to $6 million). At least two-thirds of the capital should be paid in prior to the commencement of operations.

The Agency as already indicated would be fundamentally a public service institution performing governmental functions and not seeking a profit. In order to be assured of sufficient income to cover its expenses, however, the Agency should make a reasonable charge to Government for services, such as conversion of foreign funds into local currency and transfer of money within the country. Thus the Agency would be free to act as a public service institution solely on the basis of effectively performing its functions for the benefit of the Government and the public, and the management would not have to decide the Agency's policy according to whether its operations would be a source of gain.

Direction and Administration. The Agency should be under control of a Board of Directors chosen in such manner as to provide for the best practicable consideration of Saudi Arabia's true interests. The Minister of Finance should be President. The Governor of the Agency should be ex officio a member. The Board should be a small body with not more than five Directors. Each Director, in the wording of Article 33 of the Charter of the Reserve Bank of Peru, should be "considered to be a representative of the Nation as a whole, and shall always vote for what he considers to be the general public interest."

Selection of a Governor with proper qualifications is of utmost importance. The Agency's work will involve many important problems that are highly specialized and technical. These include such matters as coinage and issuance of coins and maintenance of their internal and external value; operation of monetary reserve funds, handling foreign exchange sales so as not to disturb the local market; regulation of commercial banks, foreign exchange dealers and money changers as may be found appropriate; and economic research to aid the government in determining and carrying out its economic and financial policies.

In view of the very specialized qualifications needed for this work, the Saudi Arabian Government may wish to do as a number of other countries have done, and engage from outside of Saudi Arabia a well-qualified man and entrust to him the operation of the Agency in accordance with general policies to be specified in its charter and under the general supervision of the Board of Directors. One of his most important duties would be to train a staff of Saudi Arabian nationals so that they can gradually assume increasing responsibility with technical competence and in the spirit of public service.

The Agency might have three departments:

Treasury Department — for fiscal agency functions.
Currency Department — for monetary affairs.
Research Department — for economic and financial research.

These departments would correspond with the functions already outlined. Care should be taken to avoid over-organization. Of course the personnel should be carefully chosen. Because of the lack of trained Saudi Arabs, men from other Arab states will have to be employed to some extent as staff, pending the results of a program of training.

Reports and Audit. The Agency should render to the Government through the Ministry of Finance monthly reports of its operations. The Agency should be subject to audit by an auditor appointed by the Government.

Arthur N. Young
Financial Adviser

III. ROYAL DECREE SANCTIONING THE CHARTER OF THE SAUDI ARABIAN MONETARY AGENCY

No. 30/4/1/1047

25 Rajab, 1371
April 20, 1952

WITH THE HELP OF GOD ALMIGHTY

We, Abdul-Aziz Ibn Abdul-Rahman Al-Faisal, King of Saudi Arabia,

Upon seeing the Decree No. 30/4/1/1046 issued 25 Rajab, 1371, and the charter for the Saudi Arabian Monetary Agency, which is attached to this order and which consists of twelve articles, and

In view of what Our Minister of Finance has submitted to Us,

We ordain the following:

The charter for the Saudi Arabian Monetary Agency referred to above and attached to this Order is hereby sanctioned, and We order putting it into effect.

CHARTER OF THE SAUDI ARABIAN MONETARY AGENCY

I. Creation and Objects

1. There is hereby created according to these regulations an institution to be called Saudi Arabian Monetary Agency, the main operating office in which it shall start its functions to be in Jidda. It shall have branches and agencies in the places where required.

2. The objects of the Agency shall be:

    (a) To strengthen the currency of Saudi Arabia and to stabilize it in relation to foreign currencies, and to avoid the losses resulting to the Government and the people from fluctuations in the exchange value of Saudi Arabian coins whose rates have not so far been fixed in relation to foreign currencies which form the major part of the Government's income.

    (b) To aid the Ministry of Finance in centralizing the receipts and expenditures of the Government in accordance with the items of the authorized budget and in controlling payments so that all branches of the Government shall abide by the budget.

II. Capital

3. The Agency shall have an authorized capital equivalent to 500,000 gold sovereigns (calculated at $12.00 and equivalent to $6,000,000). The Government shall provide the entire capital of the Agency. At least two-thirds of the capital shall be paid in prior to commencement of operations. Paid in capital shall include the value of a building or buildings and equipment which the Government may provide.

III. Operations

4. The Agency shall have the following functions in relation to currency.

   (a) To stabilize and maintain the external and internal value of the currency.
   (b) To hold and operate any monetary reserve funds as separate funds earmarked for monetary purposes only.
   (c) To buy and sell for Government account gold and silver coin and bullion.
   (d) To advise the Government about new coinage and handle the manufacture, shipment and issue of all coins; it being understood that coins would be issued only through and at the request of the Agency.
   (e) To regulate commercial banks, exchange dealers and money changers as may be found appropriate.

5. The Agency shall aid the Ministry of Finance in centralizing the receipts and expenditures of the Government in accordance with the items of the authorized budget and in controlling payments so that all branches of the Government shall abide by the budget. To that end the Agency shall have the following functions:

   (a) To receive and act as depository for all revenues including receipts from concessionaire companies, from customs, from the Haj, and from other sources, and to maintain deposit accounts under such heads as the Government through the Minister of Finance may direct.

(b) To act as agent for the Government in paying out funds for purposes duly approved by the Government through the Minister of Finance.

6. The Agency shall establish a Research Department to collect and analyze data needed to aid the Government and the Agency in formulating and carrying out financial and economic policies.

7. The Agency shall not charge any profits on its receipts and payments and shall not act in any manner which conflicts with the teachings of the Islamic law. The Agency shall not undertake any of the following functions:

(a) Paying or receiving interest.

(b) Receiving private deposits.

(c) Making advances to the Government or to private parties.

(d) Engaging in trade or having an interest in any commercial, industrial or agricultural enterprise.

(c) Buying or holding fixed property except what the Agency reasonably needs for its operations.

(f) Issuing currency notes.

IV. Direction and Administration

8. The Agency shall be under the control of a Board of Directors which shall be generally responsible for its efficient administration and operation and shall have such powers as are necessary and appropriate to that end. The Board of Directors may make such rules and regulations as it may consider necessary and appropriate to the conduct of the work of the Agency in accordance with this charter. In the event that changes in this charter are found necessary, the Board of Directors shall recommend them to the Government through the Minister of Finance.

9. The Agency in the name, "Saudi Arabian Monetary Agency," shall be a corporation with continuing succession. The Agency

is authorized to take such action as may be necessary and appropriate to give effect to this charter including, but without thereby limiting its authority, authority to make contracts, to acquire and hold and pledge assets, and to incur such liabilities as are necessary and appropriate to the conduct of its operations.

10. The Board of Directors shall consist of a President, a Vice-President, a Governor of the Agency, and two other members. These shall be appointed by an order of His Majesty the King upon nomination by the Minister of Finance.

11. The Minister of Finance shall nominate the Governor of the Agency and obtain an order for his appointment from His Majesty the King. The Governor shall not be removed from office except by an order from His Majesty the King.

V. Reports and Audit

12. The Agency shall render to the Government through the Minister of Finance monthly reports of its operations. The Agency shall be subject to audit by auditors appointed by the Government.

NOTES

CHAPTER 1

1. On Wahhabism see the chapter by George Rentz, "Wahhabism and Saudi Arabia," in *The Arabian Peninsula,* ed. Derek Hopwood (London: Allen and Unwin, 1972).

2. For a good account of Ibn Saud's rise to power see David Holden and Richard Johns, *The House of Saud* (New York: Holt, Rinehart and Winston, 1981). See also H. St. John Philby, *Arabian Jubilee,* ist American ed. (New York: John Day, 1953), pp. 1–98.

3. Comments to me by retired Ambassador William J. Porter, who served in the Baghdad legation under Minister Resident Paul Knabenshue during this period.

4. H. St. John Philby, *The Heart of Arabia* (London: Constable, 1972), pp. 293–94; Elizabeth Monroe, *Philby of Arabia* (London: Faber and Faber, 1973), pp. 70, 91–93; Reader Bullard, *The Camels Must Go* (London: Faber and Faber, 1961), p. 13.

5. Philby, *Arabian Jubilee,* pp. 167–72.

6. Ibid., pp. 170–72.

7. Data supplied by Aramco in 1951.

8. Monroe, *Philby of Arabia,* pp. 212–13.

9. Foreign Relations of the United States (FRUS) 1930 III, pp. 281–84; 1933 II, pp. 986–1001. 1939 IV, pp. 824–31; 1941 III, pp. 655–56; 1942 IV, pp. 559–61; 1943 IV, pp. 830–31; 1949 VI, pp. 1573–74.

10. Especially important books are Irvine H. Anderson, *Aramco, the United States*

and Saudi Arabia: A Study of the Dynamics of Foreign Oil Policy, 1933–1950 (Princeton, N.J.: Princeton University Press, 1981); Stephen H. Longrigg, *Oil in the Middle East,* 3d ed. (New York: Oxford University Press, 1968); Elizabeth Monroe, *Britain's Moment in the Middle East, 1914–1971* (Baltimore: Johns Hopkins University Press, 1981), and *Philby of Arabia;* H. St. John Philby, *Arabian Oil Ventures* (Washington, D.C.: Middle East Institute, 1964), and *Arabian Jubilee;* and K. S. Twitchell (with Edward Jurji and R. Bayly Winder), *Saudi Arabia,* 3d ed. (Princeton, N.J.: Princeton University Press, 1958).

11. Philby, *Arabian Oil Ventures,* pp. 74–75; Twitchell, op. cit., pp. 139–45.

12. Twitchell, op. cit., pp. 216–17, Longrigg, op. cit., p. 102.

13. Anderson, op. cit., p. 9.

14. Twitchell, op. cit., pp. 217–22. For an account of the very complicated oil situation then existing in the Middle East see Anderson, op. cit., pp. 10–24.

15. The fullest account of the negotiations is in Philby, *Arabian Oil Ventures,* Part III, "The California Concessions." Longrigg, op. cit., gives a brief account, pp. 106–10, as does Twitchell, op. cit., pp. 217–23. See also Monroe, *Britain's Moment in the Middle East,* pp. 102–5, 204.

16. The text of the agreements is contained in *Selected Documents of the International Petroleum Industry: Saudi Arabia—Pre-1966,* published by OPEC at Vienna (not dated).

17. Philby, *Arabian Oil Ventures;* foreword by F. A. Davies, former chairman of Aramco, pp. xi–xii.

18. FRUS 1939 IV, pp. 826–31.

19. Longrigg, op. cit., pp. 132–33; Philby, *Arabian Oil Ventures,* p. xii.

CHAPTER 2

1. Elizabeth Monroe, *Philby of Arabia* (London: Faber and Faber, 1973), p. 213; and H. St. John Philby, *Arabian Jubilee,* 1st American ed. (New York: John Day, 1953), p. 227.

2. FRUS 1941 III, p. 635; data are from Aramco in 1951.

3. FRUS 1941 III, p. 632; 1942 IV, p. 573; 1943 IV, pp. 859–60; and data from Aramco in 1951.

4. Irvine H. Anderson, *Aramco, the United States and Saudi Arabia: A Study in the Dynamics of Foreign Oil Policy, 1933–1950* (Princeton, N.J.: Princeton University Press, 1981), p. 55.

5. FRUS 1943 IV, p. 936.

6. FRUS 1941 III, pp. 638–42; 1943 IV, p. 860.

7. FRUS 1945 VIII, p. 879.

8. FRUS 1943 IV, pp. 869, 874–75, 880 ff. Reports of the Secretary of the Treasury, passim, especially for years ended June 30, 1946, pp. 86–87, and 1963, pp. 716–17.

9. FRUS 1943 IV, pp. 916–17; 1945 VIII, pp. 873 n. and 900 n.; 1947 V, p. 1335; U.S. Director of the Mint reports, 1945, p. 7; 1946, p. 3; 1948, p. 52. *Aramco*

World Magazine (September–October 1981), p. 6. For sovereign quotations from 1945 see *Middle East Journal,* vol. 7, no. 3 (1963), pp. 364–65.

10. FRUS 1944 IV, pp. 757–59.

11. FRUS 1945 VIII, pp. 869, 878, 890, 905–17, 926, 952, 961–62.

12. FRUS 1941 III, pp. 643, 645–49.

13. FRUS 1943 IV, pp. 864–66.

14. FRUS 1943 IV, pp. 876–82, 901, 919.

15. FRUS 1941 III, pp. 631, 655–56; 1943 IV, pp. 848–81, 919; 1945 VIII, p. 941.

16. FRUS 1944 IV, pp. 719, 732, 754.

17. FRUS 1943 IV, 848, 877, 916, 919; 1944 V, pp. 683, 695, 708.

18. For a full account of these meetings see David Holden and Richard Johns, *The House of Saud* (New York: Holt, Rinehart and Winston, 1981), pp. 135–40.

19. Winston Churchill, *Triumph and Tragedy* (Cambridge, Mass.: Houghton Mifflin, 1953), pp. 397–98.

20. FRUS 1945 VIII, p. 9.

21. FRUS 1950 V, pp. 57–61.

CHAPTER 3

1. FRUS 1944 V, pp. 757–59.

2. FRUS 1950 V, pp. 58–60, 77, 97, 111–13.

3. FRUS 1950 V, pp. 96, 108, 112–13, 118–21. The decrees were officially published in Arabic and English by Imp. Misr. S.A.E., Cairo. The text of the agreement of December 30, 1950, was given to me by Aramco. A French translation was published in *Le Commerce du Levant,* Beirut, August 29, 1951.

4. Reports of the Export-Import Bank, 1945–55, passim; FRUS 1945 VIII, pp. 981–83; 1946 VII, pp. 741–44; 1948 V, Part I, pp. 226–27, 242.

5. FRUS 1950 V, pp. 1124–25.

6. FRUS 1950 V, pp. 1192–93.

7. This and part of the following account are based on notes of the author's briefing at the State Department in 1951.

8. FRUS 1948 V, Part I, pp. 238–43.

9. FRUS 1948 V, Part I, p. 238 n.

10. FRUS 1948 V, Part I, pp. 248–49.

11. Ibid.

12. Besides sources herein especially noted, data concerning the Eddy-Mikesell mission and events that followed prior to my arrival in Saudi Arabia in 1951 were supplied to me by the State and Treasury departments and Aramco in connection with preparation for my mission.

13. For other figures of coinage see *Middle East Journal,* vol. 7, no. 3 (1953), p. 363. The figures there do not include 15 million riyals coined in India in 1941 and 1943 (FRUS 1941 III, p. 639; 1943 IV, p. 858).

14. FRUS 1950 V, p. 1196.

CHAPTER 4

1. Reader Bullard, *The Camels Must Go* (London: Faber and Faber, 1961), p. 132.
2. An excellent account of Jidda's history and its condition in the early 1950s is in Richard H. Sanger, *The Arabian Peninsula* (Ithaca, N.Y.: Cornell University Press, 1954), chap. 1. Elizabeth Monroe, *Philby of Arabia*, tells graphically of conditions in the 1920s (London: Faber and Faber, 1973), p. 153.
3. Derek Hopwood, ed., *The Arabian Peninsula* (London: Allen and Unwin, 1961), pp. 26–27. See also books listed in Chapter 1, note 2.
4. Monroe, op. cit., p. 67.
5. Bullard, op. cit., p. 198.
6. FRUS 1950 V, pp. 1169–72.
7. Sanger, op. cit., pp. 3–4.
8. Saudi newspaper, *Al-Madinah al-Munawwarah,* August 25, 1952.

CHAPTER 5

1. Translated from *Al-Bilad al-Saudiya,* 28 Sha'ban, 1371 (May 22, 1952).

CHAPTER 6

1. H. St. John Philby, *Arabian Oil Ventures* (Washington, D.C.: Middle East Institute, 1964), pp. 30–35; K. S. Twitchell, *Saudi Arabia,* 3rd ed. (Princeton, N.J.: Princeton University Press, 1958), pp. 245–51.
2. Philby comments about some of the monetary difficulties of these years in *Arabian Jubilee,* 1st American ed. (New York: John Day, 1953), pp. 54, 82, 149–50, 166–69. On coinage and currency see also R. B. Winder, *Saudi Arabia in the Nineteenth Century* (New York: Octagon Books, 1980), p. 89, n. 4 and p. 214.
3. Handy and Harman, *The Silver Market in 1961,* p. 28.
4. For an earlier departure of Najib Bey Salihah over financial matters see Robert Lacey, *The Kingdom* (London: Hutchinson, 1981), p. 265.

CHAPTER 7

1. *Middle East Journal,* vol. 7 (1953), p. 550.
2. Letters from A. N. McLeod to the author January 5 and February 10, 1954; Saudi Arabian Monetary Agency annual report, 1977, pp. ii–iii.
3. Letters from A. N. McLeod, January 5 and February 10, 1954.
4. Letter of April 1, 1955, from John Parke Young to me, reporting a conversation with Blowers.
5. U.S. Department of Commerce, World Trade Information Service, Part I, No. 55–58, *Economic Reports,* "Economic Developments in Saudi Arabia 1954," p. 3.

6. Handy and Harman, annual reports, 1951, p. 23, and 1955, pp. 6–9, 31.

7. Handy and Harman, annual reports, 1955, p. 14, and 1956, p. 14.

8. Handy and Harman, 1961 report, p. 28.

9. SAMA, first annual report, 1380 (1960–61), p. 3.

10. I gave a full account of financial developments from 1952 to 1960 in "Financial Reforms in Saudi Arabia," *Middle East Journal*, vol. 14, no. 4 (1960), pp. 466–69. See also an article by H. St. John Philby, "Saudi Arabia: The New Statute of the Council of Ministers," *Middle East Journal*, vol. 12, no. 3 (1958), pp. 318–23. These events are also described in the Monetary Agency's first annual report, for 1960–61, p. 3.

11. Budget figures for 1952–53 are from my records, and for 1959 and thereafter from SAMA annual reports and *Statistical Summaries*, passim.

12. R. H. Sanger, *The Arabian Peninsula* (Ithaca, N.Y.: Cornell University Press, 1954), p. 55.

13. SAMA annual report, 1397 (1977), p. iv.

14. Figure for 1953 from author's records; for 1982, from *International Financial Statistics* (February 1982), p. 341.

15. SAMA annual report, 1977, pp. i–ix.

CHAPTER 8

1. Appendix I, Table 1, and SAMA annual report, 1981, p. 12.

2. SAMA annual reports, passim, and Appendix I, Table 1.

3. *International Financial Statistics*, passim.

4. *Wall Street Journal*, April 7, 1982, p. 31.

5. *Al-Madinah al-Munawnarah*, August 28, 1952.

6. For figures of actual costs see SAMA annual report, 1980, p. 27. The U.S. Treasury Department published an 81-page summary of its 663-page report: "United States–Saudi Arabian Joint Commission: Summary of Saudi Arabian Five Year Development Plan, 1975–1980" (Washington, D.C., 1975). This showed details and estimated costs of the first two plans.

7. This plan has been published in Saudi Arabia. Important data are contained in an address by Bonnie Pounds of the Treasury Department, which has helped through the United States–Saudi Arabian joint economic commission, at the American-Arab Association for Commerce and Industry at New York, June 26, 1980. See also *Wall Street Journal*, March 18, 1980, p. 27; *Business Week*, March 31, 1980, pp. 52–59.

8. SAMA annual report, 1979, pp. 1, 161; 1980 pp. 65–66; *International Financial Statistics*, passim.

9. SAMA annual report, 1981, pp. 85–86, 95.

10. See "Science: The Islamic Legacy," in *Aramco World Magazine* (May–June 1982).

11. SAMA annual report, 1981, pp. 97–99.

12. Ibid., pp. 92–93.

13. See *Aramco World Magazine*, which devoted its May–June 1979 issue to "America as Alma Mater."

14. For a detailed account of OPEC's formation and activities through the crisis climaxed in 1973–74 see the chapter by Zuhayr Mikdashi, "The OPEC Process," in Raymond Vernon, ed., *The Oil Crisis* (New York: W.W. Norton, 1976), pp. 203–15.

15. U.S. Senate, *Hearings before the Subcommittee on Multilateral Corporations, Multilateral Petroleum Companies,* 1974, Part VII, pp. 506–9, 515–16.

16. For a detailed account of these events see Robert B. Stobaugh's chapter, "The Oil Companies in the Crisis," in Vernon, op. cit., pp. 179–202.

17. Oil revenues are from *OPEC Annual Statistical Bulletin 1980*. For 1981 the amount of the 1980 figure is added. Figures of GDP and population are from *World Almanac, 1982*.

18. National Foreign Assessment Center, CIA, *International Energy Statistical Review,* December 22, 1981, p. 1.

19. Department of Energy, Energy Information Administration, *Weekly Petroleum Status Report,* April 9, 1982, p. 23. American consumer prices increased 211 percent from 1973 to 1981. See *International Financial Statistics,* passim.

20. Appendix I, Tables 3 and 7; *International Energy Statistical Review,* December 22, 1981, p. 1.

21. Appendix I, Tables 7 and 8.

22. Appendix I, Table 7.

23. See Appendix I, Tables 7 and 8, and statement by OPEC's president, Mani Sa'id Utaybah, oil minister of the United Arab Emirates, quoted in *Los Angeles Times*, April 22, 1982.

24. For figures and analysis for 1973–78 see Robert M. Dunn, Jr., "Exchange Rates, Payments Adjustments, and OPEC," *Essays in International Finance,* No. 137, (Princeton, N.J.: Department of Economics, Princeton University, December 1979). For later figures see *Business Week*, March 22, 1982, p. 70.

25. Figures for 1973–80 from IMF, *World Economic Outlook, 1980,* p. 102; and World Bank, *World Debt Tables* (EC-167/81), December 1981, pp. xx–xxiii. The estimate for 1981 is derived from figures in a staff study, *Development Prospects of the Capital-Surplus Oil-Exporting Countries,* World Bank Staff Working Paper No. 483, August 1981, p. 48. This is not an official document of the World Bank. See also *IMF Survey,* December 14, 1981, p. 390.

26. *IMF Survey,* March 5, 1979, pp. 65, 75–77; August 6, 1979, p. 242; and October 13, 1980, pp. 299–300, 310; IMF *Annual Report 1981,* pp. 172–87. Also data from SAMA.

27. Data from SAMA; *Wall Street Journal,* December 17, 1981, p. 1.

28. Robert Mabro, "OPEC, Oil Nationalism, and the U.S. Elephant," *Petroleum Intelligence Weekly*, April 30, 1979, p. 3.

29. FRUS 1947 V, p. 1336.

30. For a good discussion of Saudi Arabia's foreign policy and security see Wil-

liam B. Quandt, *Saudi Arabia in the 1980s: Foreign Policy, Security, and Oil* (Washington, D.C.: The Brookings Institution, 1981).

31. Meetings of June 28–29, 1982, reported in *Wall Street Journal,* June 29, p. 27, and June 30, 1982, p. 27; *Los Angeles Times,* June 30, 1982, Part I, p. 10.

32. For a good account of this episode see the chapter by James Buchan, ''The Return of the Ikhwan,'' in David Holden and Richard Johns, *The House of Saud* (New York: Holt, Rinehart and Winston, 1981), pp. 511–26.

INDEX

Aba al-Khayl, Finance Minister Mohammed, 120

Abd al-Aziz ibn Abd al-Rahman ibn Faysal al-Saud (Ibn Saud):
unification of Saudi Arabia, 1-4, 30; talents and characteristics, 19, 22, 42-44; British aid to, 4-5, 12, 14-17; defeat of Husayn (Hussein), 2-4, 45; becomes ruler of Hijaz, 4; King of Saudi Arabia, 4; early financial problems, 4-5, 7; aid from Soviets, 5; seeks U.S. recognition, 5; aid from and support by the United States, 11-17;
favors development, 7, 19, 104; invites Twitchell to arrange oil exploration, 6, 7; doubt about oil prospects, 7; grant of oil concessions, 7-9; presided at loading first oil tanker, 9; borrowed against oil revenue, 5, 12, 20; and having a financial adviser, 15, 27, 29; meeting with President Roosevelt, 15-16, 27; and American-British rivalry, 15-17;
and deficit spending, 19, 21-23, 52; and railway, 20; and budget, 23; and American policy re Israel, 16, 27; abolished pilgrim dues, 51; and *Ramadan,* 36; prohibited alcoholic drinks, 38; travels between Riyadh and Taif, 41; received financial adviser at Taif, 40-43; gift of airplane from Roosevelt, 41; and *majlis,* 44; and Shaykh Abd Allah Sulayman (Suleiman), 44-45;
desire for a national bank, 55; palace of, 41-42; sons of, 60; and creation of Saudi Arabian Monetary Agency, 58, 61-64; audiences of financial adviser with, 40-43, 61, 63-64, 75; and currency problems, 75; and Islamic religion, 36, 43, 104; and coinage, 76; and foreign policy, 115, 119; death of, 22, 43

Abu-Izz al-Din, Fu'ad (Izzadine), 51

Accounting: experts requested, 27; named, 31; work of experts, 50-51

Acheson, Secretary of State Dean, 30

Afghanistan, 118

Agriculture, 45, 48, 93, 105-6

Airborne Warning and Control Systems (AWACS), 118, 121

Al-Attas, Husayn (Alatas), 47

Alcoholic liquors, prohibition of, 38

Al-Faqih, Ambassador Asad, 31

Algeria, 131

Ali, Anwar, Governor of Monetary Agency: appointment, 96; and reforms, 96-98; death, 98

Al-Khalidi, Rasem Bey, 74

NEW YORK UNIVERSITY
STUDIES IN NEAR EASTERN CIVILIZATION
NUMBER 8

General Editor
Bayly Winder

ALSO IN THIS SERIES

NEW YORK UNIVERSITY STUDIES IN NEAR EASTERN CIVILIZATION

The participation of the New York University Press in the University's commitment to Near Eastern Studies provides Americans and others with new opportunities for understanding the Near East. Concerned with those various peoples of the Near East who, throughout the centuries, have dramatically shaped many of mankind's most fundamental concepts and who have always had high importance in practical affairs, this series, New York University Studies in Near Eastern Civilization, seeks to publish important works in this vital area. The purview will be broad, open to varied approaches and historical periods, including the range of social scientific approaches. It will, however, be particularly receptive to work in two areas that reflect the University and that may have received insufficient attention elsewhere. These are literature and art. Furthermore, taking a stand that may be more utilitarian than that of some other publications, the series will welcome translations of important Near Eastern literature. In this way, an audience, unacquainted with the languages of the Near East, will be able to deepen its knowledge of the cultural achievements of Near Eastern peoples.

Bayly Winder
General Editor